AN ELECTRIC STORM

Daphne, Delia and the BBC Radiophonic Workshop

Ned Netherwood

Published in 2015 by Obverse Books
Cover Design © Cody Schell

Text © Ned Netherwood, 2015

With special thanks to Ray White for help, assistance and encouragement beyond the call of duty, Stuart for asking me to write this, Sonic Boom, Elizabeth Parker, Brian Hodgson, Clive Graham, Alice, Leslie & Mick at Goldsmiths, University of London, David Butler at Manchester University, countless others for their enthusiasm and support which has helped more than they can imagine. Love to Gena, Otis and Willow, of course.

Ned Netherwood has asserted his right to be identified as the author of this Work in accordance with the Copyright, Designs and Patents Act 1988.

All rights reserved. No part of this publication may be reproduced, stored in a retrieval system, or in any form or by any means, without the prior permission in writing of the publisher, nor be otherwise circulated in any form of binding, cover or e-book other than which it is published and without a similar condition including this condition being imposed on the subsequent publisher.

If not specifically noted, all correspondence from and to Daphne Oram comes from The Oram Collection at Goldsmiths, University of London

CONTENTS

Introduction 5
Chapter One: "I hoped afresh for a miracle in sound"
.... 9
Chapter Two: "A Herd of Rhinoceroses" 30
Chapter Three – "Fag-ends and Lollipops" 45
Chapter Four: 'It was just the Pet Shop Boys and myself' 63
Chapter Five – "Shall I give you the key then?" 77
Chapter Six – "A cross between a Meccano set and a chip shop" 86
Chapter Seven – "Ace performers with a Razor Blade" 96
Part Two: The Complete Reviews 105

Part One: The Radiophonic Workshop

Introduction

"A 'workshop' for producing sounds, partly by electronic oscillators and partly by trickery with conventional sounds recorded on tape, has been set up by the B.B.C at their Maida Vale studios. It is being used to provide an imaginative background to drama productions which cannot be obtained from ordinary music or from the stock-in-trade of sound effects."[1]

With this brief, and slightly stilted, announcement in the Times newspaper in late May 1958, the BBC Radiophonic Workshop was unveiled before the eyes of the world. The first such dedicated electronic music studio in the United Kingdom, the Workshop swiftly established itself at the forefront of experimental sound creation across Europe and beyond.

Initially the brainchild of Desmond Briscoe and Daphne Oram, the Workshop provided a refuge for many of the pioneers of electronic sound in the country, including Brian Hodgson, Roger Limb, Malcolm Clarke, Delia Derbyshire and Maddelana Fagandini, each of whom went on to make a major contribution to the field. The first ever radiophonic play broadcast in Britain, the theme tune for *Doctor Who*, entire albums of neo-folk, psychedelia, spoken word and noise, jingles for Lego, instant tea and the Kia-Ora soft drink - the Radiophonic Workshop was responsible for an enormous range of sound effects and musical pieces. Without them, it's fair to say, the aural landscape of three decades worth of UK radio and television would be entirely different – and far less interesting.

In the first half of the book you hold in your hand, author Ned Netherwood traces the birth and growth of the Workshop, highlighting its main practitioners and their achievements, before chronicling its eventual downfall in the late eighties, as Producer Choice and Birtism destroyed much of what made the BBC unique. Speaking to many of the people who were there, he builds a picture of an institution which all but stumbled over a fabulously unexpected and tremendously useful resource, but which in the end perhaps did not truly appreciate what it had.

In the second half of the book, and for the first time in book form, the author listens to and reviews the entirety of the Workshop's output, and much recorded afterwards by the best known faces from Maida Vale. From flex-discs, 7" singles and promotional cds all the way to multi-volume retrospectives, everything is in here, and everything has been weighted and judged by a life-long fan of the Workshop.

Chapter One: "I hoped afresh for a miracle in sound"

It's impossible properly to consider the formation of the BBC Radiophonic Workshop, without first very briefly exploring the origins of the BBC itself, and examining the cultural precedents that inspired it.

Founded in 1922 as the British Broadcasting Company Ltd by the General Post Office and a consortium of six companies involved in radio manufacturing, including Marconi and General Electric, the new company was initially formed to broadcast experimental radio services, but the partnership quickly broke down over the thorny issue of profit.

Government regulators had opposed advertising in the belief it would compromise quality, so a license fee for radio owners was recommended. Set at an initial cost of ten shillings, the license quickly superseded the commission the BBC had previously received on the sale of radios from approved manufacturers as its primary source of funding, meaning that the pernicious effect of commercials could be avoided altogether. However, the Post Office were not keen on doing the fee collections and the financial losses displeased the radio manufacturers. In 1925, therefore, the BBC's first general manager, John Reith, proposed a new charter to the government which came into being on January 1st 1927, for a BBC independent of any government or corporation.

In this unique position, the BBC was free to concentrate on quality and variety without having to please a sponsor or tow any particular party line. Freed from the pressures of competition and commercialism, the BBC dedicated itself to broadcasting a wide ranging body of work. They aimed to produce something for all British people, from all walks of life, to – in Reith's own words – "inform, educate, entertain". They created a diverse dramatic and factual output alongside music broadcasting, with a complete monopoly on official radio broadcasting until the first commercial stations were permitted to broadcast in the 1970s. It was into this world of innovation, invention and experimentation that broadcast electronic music was born.

The idea of a broadcaster having a dedicated electronic music studio was not a BBC – or even British - innovation. In fact, the BBC was somewhat behind the times. Just over two hundred miles away, across the Channel, France's national broadcaster, Radiodiffusion-Télévision Française, had their own Studio d'Essai.

Studio d'Essai was originally a centre for the resistance movement during World War II and went on to be responsible for the first broadcasts from liberated Paris. Here, after the war, the French composer and theoretician Pierre Schaeffer [1910-1995] developed what was to become known as *musique concrète*.

Musique Concrète had as its goal the creation of a form of music which did not take as its building blocks the traditional boundaries of score, melody and tonality, but instead posited a form based on the manipulation of natural sounds, stripped of their original intent and repurposed – in Schaffer's own words – as *"sound fragments that exist in reality and that are considered as discrete and complete sound objects"*[2] String these sound objects together and you have music, Schaeffer stated in 1948.[3]

It was also at Studio d'Essai that the French pioneered the concept of the studio as instrument, experimenting with sampling, sound looping, mechanical reverberation and sound manipulation. Shaeffer and his colleague Pierre Henry used tape recorders to record sound objects which they then manipulated in the studio to create new forms of music.

Electronic music was still in its infancy, however. Although the first electronic instrument, the theremin, had been patented some thirty years earlier in 1928, it had failed to make any significant impact on popular music (at least until 1966 when it appeared on the Beach Boys' single "Good Vibrations").

Yet Studio d'Essai was not alone in its electronic music output. The composer Karlheinz Stockhausen [1928-2007] visited in 1952, initially simply recording percussion instruments, but by December of that year the twenty-four year old German had composed his first electroacoustic piece, 'Étude'. Stockhausen later described the process:

"First I recorded six sounds of variously prepared low piano strings struck with an iron beater, using a tape speed of 76.2 centimetres per second. After that, I copied each sound many times and, with scissors, cut off the attack of each

sound ... Several of these pieces were spliced together to form a tape loop, which was then transposed to certain pitches using a transposition machine. A few minutes of each transposition were then recorded on separate tapes."[4]

An indication of the limited access each composer had to the valuable machinery of the studio, and the often difficult working practices such limited exposure encouraged, can be gained from Stockhausen's description of his own methods at the time.

"I was only allowed to have the studio with a technician for a few hours each week. Therefore, I hammered a nail into my desktop at the student hostel, laid a metal tape hub on the nail, fastened a ruler horizontally onto the desk in front of me, and placed a series of hubs with modulated tapes and one hub with leader tape next to each other at the rear of the desk. Then I cut many short pieces from a roll of white splicing tape and stuck them next to each other on the edge of the desk.
    "I then chose, according to my score, one of the tapes having a certain sound transposition, measured the notated length in centimetres and millimetres, cut off that length, spliced it with a little piece of the splicing tape onto a lengthy piece of white leader tape, and wound the white tape plus the first little piece of magnetic tape around the metal hub on the nail. For this I used a pencil which was inserted into the outer hole of the hub.
    "Next, I chose another prepared tape, measured and cut off a piece, and spliced it onto the previous piece.

Whenever the score prescribed a pause, I spliced a corresponding length of white tape onto the result tape. Occasionally, my winding apparatus did not function, and tape salad was the result: I then crawled around on the floor under my desk searching for one end of the fallen tape. Once found, the confusion of the entangled tape was unravelled with great difficulty, and it was wound around the hub again.

"When my studio time came, I synchronized two of my spliced tapes using two play-back tape recorders, recorded the sum on a third tape recorder and copied this result again – depending on the polyphony desired – on top of a further zebra-tape of bits of brown tape and little pieces of white pause."[5]

Little wonder, in view of so haphazard a working methodology, that results were not always as intended. Stockhausen, again discussing 'Etude':

"Already upon hearing two synchronized layers, and even more so hearing three or four layers, I became increasingly pale and helpless: I had imagined something completely different! On the following day, the sorcery undespairingly continued: I changed my series, chose other sequences, cut other lengths, spliced different progressions, and hoped afresh for a miracle in sound."[6]

In spite of the composer's misgivings (he also described 'Etude' as a "negative result"[7]), listening to the piece today, it is hard not to agree with musicologist Robin Maconie that "[g]iven the extraordinary technical difficulties Stockhausen had to endure, the Konkrete Etude is a very impressive achievement."[8]

So impressive, in fact, that within months Studio d'Essai's German rivals NWDR had provided studios for Stockhausen and his electronic experiments, while, in Holland, the acclaimed Dutch composer Henk Badings [1907-1987] was provided with a "more or less improvised"[9] electronic studio by Philips in 1956. From there, fellow Dutchman Edgard Varese [1883-1965] produced his critically lauded *Poeme Electronique* in 1958[10]. These endeavours were widely acclaimed in contemporary classical circles and each carried a great deal of prestige, but they had not yet caught on with the general population in either country, or in Britain.

British composer and BBC employee Daphne Oram called regularly upon the BBC, hoping to set up something similar but her ideas seemed never to catch on with the BBC music department. She had joined the BBC in 1943 at the age of 18[11], having turned down a place at the Royal Academy of Music. Her first job was as a sound balancer, making sure the sound levels remained consistent for everything broadcast on the radio[12].

It is unlikely such an opportunity would have been open to her had it not been for World War II creating a shortage of the type of young men who would normally be employed by the BBC for such work.

However, while Oram quickly made herself at

home working such technical jobs, her ideas for electronic music were not welcomed:

"I went along to the research department at Nightingale Square, to ask one of the high-up engineers there whether he would allow me some equipment and guide me technically towards this music I was imagining. But he reduced me to a very small height, and finished by saying, 'Miss. Oram, the BBC employs a hundred musicians to make all the sounds they require, thank you."

Undeterred, Daphne would stay behind at night when nobody was using the BBCs recording studios and borrow their equipment to create her own makeshift temporary studio. Here, in secret, she began to develop her own techniques and methods.[13]

1955 was a highly significant year in the evolution of BBC policy. Importantly, BBC Radio's Third Programme began to experiment more and more within the medium, with at times startling effects. The Third Programme had a remit to be the most innovative and intellectual radio station at the BBC (as opposed to the Light Programme station which broadcast light entertainment shows and popular music, and the Home Service which was mostly speech based). The Third Programme broadcast classical concerts as well as contemporary music and jazz alongside drama from the likes of Harold Pinter, Joe Orton and, most famously, Dylan Thomas with his most best-known work, *Under Milk Wood*. The producers of The Third Programme had no prejudices against electronic music but internal hostility towards the subject from within the BBC's music department, meant that they had no internal department they could commission it from in similar manner to their continental counterparts. The BBC's music department consisted purely of traditional instruments and musicians.

Even so, in 1955 the Third Programme broadcast a play with an electronic soundtrack from pioneering British electronic musician, Tristram Cary: *Japanese Fishermen*. The same year listeners could also enjoy *Nadja Etoilée* an opera originating from Studio d'Essai with some *musique concrète* from André Almuro (whose work was adapted again in 1957 when Cleverdon oversaw a translation of RTF's *Opium*, a collaboration between Almuro and Jean Cocteau) and the award-winning *Orestes*, another *musique concrète* opera. Producer Douglas Cleverdon provided brief introductions to each work in order to prepare the listener for what they were about to experience.

    The year closed with the broadcast in December of the play *Night Thoughts*, another Cleverdon production, though this time with Humphrey Searle providing a soundtrack that veered from traditional to *musique concrète* for David Gascoyne's lyrical invocation of London at night. While the BBC Music Department might have been unwilling to create such sounds, the BBC was certainly not unwilling to play them.

    The BBC's lack of electronic music facilities were felt most keenly by the Third Programme's drama department. Although the Corporation had set up a committee to look into non-traditional effects in late 1956 (initially called the Electrophonic Effects Committee, changing to Radiophonic in December 1957[14]), it was in January 1957 that a specific broadcast event highlighted their lack of facilities and prompted an increase in urgency. At that time, the BBC broadcast an exclusive script by the Irish playwright Samuel Beckett - an occasion that would prove pivotal in the drama department's case for a dedicated electronic music studio at the BBC. This was a prestigious production for the BBC as Beckett's most famous work, *Waiting For Godot* had premiered only five years earlier and this was the first time he had written especially for radio. Increasingly recognised as one of the greatest playwrights of his generation, the ears of the world would be on Beckett - and London.

However, Beckett lived in Paris and even wrote many of his plays in French. He certainly knew Studio D'Essai as they had premiered *Waiting For Godot* in an abridged form almost a year before the theatrical debut of the complete play. He must have been assuming that the Corporation had a similar electronic studio, because he told the BBC that the script, entitled *All That Fall*, called for a "rather special quality of bruitage" (tellingly he uses the French term for sound effects). When a letter was sent asking him to explain what he wanted, he wrote back:

"I find it difficult to put down my thoughts about bruitage. And I am not sure what I want to say is worth saying. I feel it might be no more than an amateur's statement of what is common radio practise. For the moment I think I had better

hold my peace. By far the best would be for us to meet, or for me to meet the bruiteur, before production, and talk it over"[15]

It became clear that his wishes were not concurrent with "common radio practise" at the BBC. The play's producer, Donald McWhinnie, had a meeting with Beckett, at which he discovered that the playwright wanted natural sound effects manipulated in unnatural ways. As a consequence, McWhinnie decided to have human actors recreate the animal noises. For the other sound effects, studio technician Desmond Briscoe - with the help of gramophone operator Norman Baines - put together the technical sound effects with only a short deadline.

The play was a critical success and won the Gold Medal from the New York International Radio Festival. However, whilst he seemed pleased with Briscoe and Bain's work, Beckett complained about the animal sound effects both before and after the production (a complaint described by Kevin Branigan, in his critical work, *Radio Beckett: Musicality in the Radio Plays of Samuel Beckett* as "*one of the few bones of contention*[16]" between author and producer). This was embarrassing for the BBC drama department, but given the facilities they had, it was a pragmatic solution.

Beckett's work can be notoriously difficult but *All That Fall* is not only among his best plays but among the best works of experimental drama ever created for radio. As is typical of Beckett, there are layers of gloom, weariness and despair but the richness of his language and the absurdity of his characters keeps the listener engaged. The play depicts an old lady in Ireland walking to the train station to meet her husband and walking home with him, meeting various unusual characters along the way. The special audio effects are not overly noticeable on her journey there but for the walk back they begin to dominate the soundscape, building a strange, macabre rhythm from their footsteps.

It should be noted that this was not the first BBC attempt at creating unusual sounds. On the BBC's Home Service, Spike Milligan regularly incorporated special sounds into *The Goon Show*, most famously using BBC custard inside one of his own socks for an infamous squelching effect, much to the horror of canteen staff.

Behind the scenes, Daphne Oram's suggestions that they launch an electronic music department was gaining considerable momentum. Oram was a natural choice to become involved in the project. Her enthusiasm and knowledge marked her out, as well as her own experiments in *musique concrète*.

It would be fair to say that Daphne Oram was not the shy, retiring type. For instance, she had been very active in trying to get the pay grade for serious music studio managers raised. Although not named in contemporary articles about the dispute, correspondence survives between Daphne and her Trade Union which show her contribution. She wrote many letters to management explaining the demands and responsibilities of the job, even though any positive result would not affect her very much, as she appears to have received a rapid succession of promotions through the department, judging by the stack of change in salary notices in the Oram Collection at Goldsmiths, University of London.[17]

However in 1955 and 1956 Oram began to receive rejections for the positions for which she applied. On 26th July 1954, she failed even to make the short list of candidates for the role of Assistant in the music programmes department. Only in 1956 did Oram's career begin to look up again, as she was thanked by Malcolm Garrard in his report to BBC management on the viability of setting up an electronic sound studio, alongside Douglas Cleverdon, Tom Eckersley and André Almuró of R.T.F.[18]

In early 1957 she was given leave from studio management to create special sound for Val Gielgud's production of *Prometheus Unbound*. Oram's friend Madeau Stewart had suggested her for the job and collaborated with her on it. Sadly, at the time of writing, the play and its soundtrack is missing from the archives.

In March 1957 BBC management put together a committee to discuss the practicalities of founding an electronic music studio and what form it should take. The term "radiophonic" was used instead of *musique concrète* at the request of the BBC music department who were insistent that what was created must not be referred to as "music". This diplomatic compromise did nothing to stem the hostility from the BBC's music department who wrote many memos critical of the project. Bernard Keefe and Frank Wade from the BBC's Music Department expressed concerns that certain individuals just wanted "a toy to play with" and even went as far as to criticise the German electronic tradition that was being cited as the example the BBC should move towards. They proposed that the drama department could make do with an electric organ to provide all their sound effects. It was entirely due to the support of the drama department that matters were allowed to move forward[19]. Oram submitted a wealth of information to the committee and provided technology updates, not to mention compiling a list of commercially available music that signposted the direction she wanted the studio to take[20].

Meanwhile, Desmond Briscoe's next major project was to create the sound effects for *The Disagreeable Oyster* by Giles Cooper, another playwright strongly behind the Radiophonic project (his *Under the Loofah Tree* was the first officially commissioned play for the newly-formed Workshop). This play had a troubled history, having been rejected by the Home Service for being too surreal, then initially rejected by the Third Programme for being too mainstream. However, a decision was made to produce the play for the Third Programme, but incorporating sound effects, with Donald McWhinnie once again producing the show and Briscoe providing sound manipulation. The play received little coverage but where it did, it was well received – Roy Curtis-Bramwell has suggested that listeners reacted especially positively to the humour in the radiophonic work[21] (for instance, the way in which a baker's bell becomes a train whistle, matching a similar change in scene).

The next radio play to receive such special sound was *The Kraken Wakes*. Mystery surrounds the precise roles of the personnel involved, as Desmond Briscoe was credited as the arranger, but among Daphne Oram's papers is an annotated script of the play, alongside intricate notes on sounds, durations and effects. It is also listed on an undated note by Daphne titled "Radiophonic Acitvities to date[22]".

Producer McWhinnie commissioned Frederick Bradnum to write *Private Dreams and Public Nightmares* which was billed as a "Radiophonic Poem" and broadcast in October 1957. This work was created specifically for special effects and this time Desmond Briscoe definitely worked alongside Daphne Oram. Whilst Bradnum was a well-established and respected writer of radio drama, he in no way approached Beckett in terms of talent or fame. He wrote many well-loved radio dramas but it would be fair to say that this was not one of them. *Private Dreams and Public Nightmares* is a work that has cultural significance only in the field of sound and radiophonics.

The words and phrases uttered are nothing but fodder for Briscoe and Oram's talents. A few actors melodramatically utter a handful of rather meaningless phrases such as "what is it that holds me suspended in the air?" while heavily distorted sounds howl and groan in the background. People begin bellowing and sounds shriek. Everything sounds dark and hellish but ultimately directionless. The listener is more enthralled by the effects than the words. Every voice is treated differently and they rise and fall out of the sound mix, displaying the tape manipulation skills of Briscoe and Oram vividly but Bradnum's talents are not at all well represented. To be frank, speeding up people's voices is always going to make the listener think of The Chipmunks no matter what ominous nonsense you have them bellow. However its saving graces are its brevity (only nineteen minutes long) and its technical excellence.

The primary impact of the new special sound imposing itself in a dominant position over the actual words was a sudden awareness of the techniques in play. While the modern, informed listener can detect the subtle work on previous productions such as *All The Fall*, nobody could mistake *Private Dreams And Public Nightmares* for anything other than a bombardment of sound manipulation. Much as Douglas Cleverdon had done in 1955 (and possibly in light of the bemused audience reaction to an earlier, non-introduced BBC radiophonic poem, *Opium*), Donald McWhinnie put together a spoken introduction explaining what was about to happen, verging on an warning and effectively admitting that the work about to begin was more about effects than text:

"This program is an experiment, an exploration. It has been put together with enormous enthusiasm with equipment designed for other purposes. It's not a masterpiece, not even a minor one, and it's not a stunt. We think it is worth broadcasting as a perfectly serious first attempt to find out whether we can convey a new kind of emotional and intellectual experience by means of what we call Radiophonic effects"[23]

Oddly, though with a refreshing honesty, the BBC press release for the show from October 7th opens with a quote from McWhinnie "*Not a masterpiece - not even a minor one*"[24]. In a letter to a friend, Daphne Oram recalled the attendees of the press conference:

"I think they found the prog rather gruesome and they don't think much of the poem (nor do I!) but they certainly found the sounds most interesting. I agree with them that it is a pity that we could not have done something beautiful instead of horrible for our first effort[25]*"*

Private Dreams and Public Nightmares was nothing short of a showcase for radiophonic effects, designed to support the case for the creation of a dedicated electronic sound studio. It succeeded in creating a surge of interest in Radiophonic sound around the BBC's many departments and, in the words of audio historian Sean Street led to *"a major new creative force that would redefine sonic possibilities across a range of media"*[26]. In retrospect, the formation of the Workshop was now inevitable and the need for assured quality plain. An interesting memo sent from the technical department to producer Robin Midgley on 5th December 1957 reflected the mood in the BBC.

"We have looked into every possible way of providing staff to help create the radiophonic effects you would like. Unfortunately, Miss Oram will be working on John Gibson's production at this time and, due to pressure of programmes, we are unable to release anyone else. As we feel that work

of this kind must be of the highest quality, it would be unwise to allocate anyone insufficiently au fait with this medium."[27]

Daphne Oram and Radiophonic events were clearly in demand. Her next big radiophonic project was for television, an adaption of the play *Amphitryon 38* by the French dramatist Jean Giraudoux. Her score was made using a sine wave oscillator, tape recorder and some filters of her own design, rather than manipulating existing sounds. It was the first piece of all-electronic music made at the BBC. Sadly, like much from that era of British television, the programme is lost and only a fragment of the soundtrack survives.

Another pioneer working with the BBC radio drama department was the writer Jeremy Sandford [1930-2003], who wrote a radio play called *The Quinquaphone* for which he was credited with both text and "quinquaphone music[28]". Sandford went on to find fame with the television play *Cathy Come Home*, the debut of director Ken Loach. His own contribution to the story was almost forgotten until a reference to Sandford's work appeared in Daphne Oram's correspondence with the BBC in 1983, in which she complains he had been written out of BBC history[29]. Oram definitively describes Sandford's musical contribution as *musique concrète*.

On the 22nd May 1958, the BBC formally announced the formation of the Radiophonic Workshop. At its inception, the Workshop saw Briscoe and Oram joined by technicians Dickie Bird and Madeau Stewart.

Oram posted a quotation from Francis Bacon's *The New Atlantis* on the wall. This was a novel published around 1627 in which Bacon describes a group of sailors finding a mythical Pacific island where a perfect society exists. Less a story than a detailed description of Bacon's own concept of Utopia, Daphne Oram highlighted one rather apt quote wherein the inhabitants tell the sailors:

"We have also sound-houses, where we practise and demonstrate all sounds, and their generation. We have harmonies which you have not, of quarter-sounds, and lesser slides of sounds. Diverse instruments of music likewise to you unknown, some sweeter than any you have, together with bells and rings that are dainty and sweet. We represent small sounds as great and deep; likewise great sounds extenuate and sharp; we make diverse tremblings and warblings of sounds, which in their original are entire. We represent and imitate all articulate sounds and letters, and the voices and notes of beasts and birds. We have certain helps which set to the ear do further the hearing greatly. We have also diverse strange and artificial echoes, reflecting the voice many times, and as it were tossing it: and some that give back the voice louder than it came, some shriller, and some deeper; yea, some rendering the voice differing in the letters or articulate sound from that they receive. We have also means to convey sounds in trunks and pipes, in strange lines and distances."

These sentiments could well serve as the mission statement of the Radiophonic Workshop through its entire existence. In fact, the quotation stayed with the Workshop far beyond Oram's brief time there – and the full quote was even used on the sleeve notes of the Workshop's 1983 compilation *Sound House - Music from the BBC Radiophonic Workshop*.

As 1958 continued, however, Oram quickly encountered problems. She had hoped for an electronic music studio along the lines of the continental ones which had inspired her, but the Workshop's remit was solely to create sound for other people's productions. She was also told that after six months she would have to leave the Workshop for her own mental well-being as it was feared it would be detrimental to be exposed to such sounds for so long[30]!

Why this did not apply to Briscoe is not made completely clear but was suggested by Daphne Oram, admittedly many years later in 1983, that he was still dividing his time between drama studio work and the Workshop, and would not have been there constantly for any substantial period of time. Frustrated, Oram wrote a letter of resignation on November 1st 1958 stating that "I wish to spend my energies in certain fields of work and these fields are not continuously open to me within the Corporation. I now have arranged to pursue these activities outside."

She was contracted to give three months notice so it was not until the end of January 1959 that she left the BBC. On her departure, the Director-General of the BBC, Sam Jacob, wrote to thank her for her service and "*especially for the recent experimental work in the*

Radiophonic Workshop with which you have been associated[31]."

By default, Desmond Briscoe now found himself in charge of the Workshop. Madeau Stewart, who had been working as technical support to Daphne Oram, quit the Workshop too, out of loyalty, and was replaced by Dick Mills. Mills, who would go on to be the longest serving member of the Workshop, leaving only forty-five years later in 1993, went on to create the sound effects for every *Doctor Who* story bar two serials from 1972 until its cancellation in 1989. His initial job was to look after the equipment but before long he was creating work including a particularly popular flatulence sound for *The Goons'* Major Bloodnok.

However, Desmond Briscoe was concerned that the Workshop could end up becoming a sound department for the Goons[32] and he would spend the rest of his days taking orders from Spike Milligan[33]. In the end, the Workshop only provided the comedy team with two sound effects then flatly refused to provide any more. Spike Milligan would later go on to publicly blame Briscoe for the demise of the *Goon Show*[34].

Although BBC radio's Third Programme continued to commission work from the Radiophonic Workshop, television began to play an increasing role. Briscoe and Mills provided sounds for the classic serial science-fiction serial *Quatermass and the Pit*, broadcast from 22 December 1958 to 26 January 1959. This, the third Quatermass serial, was both a critical and commercial hit.

Watched by over eleven million people at its peak, the show is still widely regarded as a classic today.

The Radiophonic Workshop's contribution was to create terrifying, alien sounds for the show. The show had a more traditional soundtrack taken from Trevor Duncan's library music with the addition of what was described as special sound from the Workshop. Briscoe, with assistance from Dick Mills, created sound effects and unnerving atmospheres which were cut to disc and played out in the studio, this being the era when television drama was acted out live rather than recorded for later transmission.

Prior to *Quatermass and the Pit*, the Workshop's output had been heard only by those with an interest in "high culture". Afterwards, whilst neither the Workshop nor Briscoe appeared in the credits, the existence of electronic sound had entered the consciousness of the general public.

Radiophonics had arrived.

Chapter Two: "A Herd of Rhinoceroses"

The sixties were a vintage decade for the Radiophonic Workshop. Television called on their services now, but their old friends in radio never forgot them. All manner of unusual commissions came in for radio jingles, not to mention more wonderful and unusual work from the Third Programme and others.

One instance may serve as an example of this flowering of creativity. Producer Douglas Cleverdon brought Brion Gysin to the Workshop to record a programme described as "manna from heaven" by *The Listener* magazine[35]. Gysin was the inventor of the cut-up writing technique most famously utilised by his close friend, William Burroughs. He performed what he called his "permutated poems" - so called because he would take a sentence (often the title) and then deliver every possible permutation possible but changing emphasis to constantly convey new meanings. Some of these poems, such as "Junk Is No Good Baby", seem to be just the man and a microphone, but "Pistol Poem" saw him accompanied by a very Radiophonic gunshot sound and "I Am That I Am" starts typically enough but swiftly embraces tape manipulation and surreal sound effects. Released several times on different compilations, the work is a must for anyone with an interest in the beat generation.

The growing demands for the Workshop's services required several more pairs of hands. As a consequence, many people found themselves assigned to the Workshop for three month periods, often unwillingly. It's for this reason that BBC staff like Jimmy Burnett, Dennis Morgan and John Harrison crop up on the official record as being active in the early years, but you won't find their names on any compilation of Radiophonic Music.

Some names, however, became synonymous with the Workshop.

Phil Young

One person who stayed with the Workshop only briefly but who left a small but fondly remembered body of work was Phil Young, who has three rather good tracks on the Workshop's twenty-first anniversary compilation, all dated as being created between 1959 and 1960. Although little biographical detail about Young remains on record, these are prime examples of early Radiophonic Workshop sounds and stand the test of time beautifully. His mixture of melody and strangeness is a definite precursor to Delia Derbyshire's work.

The haunting piano notes and menacing sound swirls of Young's theme for the radio programme *The Artist Speaks* suggest an encounter with sheer fear rather than the arts, for instance, while his collaboration with Maddalena Fagandini on the theme for *Science and Industry* oozes cosmic terror. Dick Mills described one particularly memorable scene from Young's time at the Workshop in a recent interview:

"Phil Young turned himself into a herd of rhinoceroses over lunch one day, which was the most liberating thing he had ever done! He didn't have key signatures and bass and treble clefs, there was complete freedom for the imagination."[36]

For reasons lost to posterity, Young's time at the Workshop was lamentably brief. The paperwork no longer exists and we cannot, therefore, be certain, but perhaps Young was a casualty of the three month rule which decreed that a placement at the Workshop should only be temporary. The rule survived until Delia Derbyshire and Brian Hodgson dug their heels in and refused to leave, so may well have impacted on Phil Young's tenure.

Maddalena Fagandini [1929 -2012]

The next notable person to join the Workshop was Maddalena Fagandini. Born in London to Italian parents, Fagandini joined the BBC as a typist but quickly moved to the production side of the Corporation, working in the drama department and using her linguistic skills for Parliamo Italiano, the first foreign-language teaching series on BBC television. Her musical background – her father sang semi-professionally, and she played the piano - helped her gain a position at the Workshop in 1959, although her work was frequently interrupted by the

BBC's need for her bi-lingual skills during events such as the 1960 Rome Olympics.

Her first big project at the Workshop was creating a soundtrack for a documentary, Outside, about a former prisoner trying to adapt to the outside world. The work was co-created with her boss, Desmond Briscoe, although when it was included on the Workshop's 21st anniversary compilation, Briscoe alone was credited!

As well as creating sound effects (the creation of which, live in the studio, was something she 'particularly loved', according to her BBC colleague, Giles Oakley[37]) another regular source of work for the Workshop was creating radio jingles for both national and regional BBC stations. One such interval piece by Fagandini called "Time Beat" caught the ear of producer George Martin who reworked it and released as a single under the pseudonym Ray Cathode. It came out on the 13th of April 1962 on Parlophone with the writing credit assigned to 'BBC Radiophonics' – the first ever release to come out of the Radiophonic Workshop. Later that same year George Martin produced another single for Parlophone, titled "Love Me Do", this time by a new signing called The Beatles.

Although she would continue working in television until the nineteen eighties, her primary area of interest in later years was in foreign language teaching (intriguingly, Giles Oakley has suggested that after the introduction of synthesisers in the mid-sixties, "*Maddalena began to lose interest in the Workshop and ... started looking elsewhere*"[38]). Even so, she was active at the Radiophonic

Workshop between 1959 and 1966 and was an early example of the strong role women played in its success.

Brian Hodgson (born 1938)

1962 saw two bright young things joining the Workshop: Brian Hodgson and Delia Derbyshire. Like many of his peers at the Workshop, Hodgson had joined the BBC as a studio manager, in his case in the drama department at the tender age of twenty five. He had previously been a stage manager in the theatre, including working on one production where he had used musique concrète recordings as the soundtrack. He also had a pre-existing curiosity about sound, having experimented with recordings made using a tape player during his R.A.F. days[39].

That said, although technology and music were to play a major part in his professional life, it was his background in drama which served him best when he found himself in charge of sound effects for *Doctor Who* throughout the nineteen sixties.

Convincingly creating the sound of the hero's time travel machine, the TARDIS, tearing its way through the fabric of time and space by dragging a key down a broken piano was just one of many Hodgson master strokes, although it is perhaps his most celebrated. His distinctive "Dalek Control Room" sound is also still used to this day every time the metal villains are depicted en masse in their own bases or craft, its monotonous, rhythmic humming a dark sonic echo of the Dalek's own technology-induced evil. These, and others, of Hodgson's sound effects can be heard in the latest episodes of the rebooted *Doctor Who*, not out of a misplaced sense of nostalgia - the show has had to reinvent itself for modern audiences and left much behind in doing so - but simply because Hodgson's work can often not be bettered. Its absence would leave a gaping hole in the show's sound which even casual viewers would notice.

Delia Derbyshire [1937-2001]

Delia Derbyshire was a Cambridge graduate with an MA in mathematics and music, which may sound an unusual academic mix, but which actually perfectly reflects her creative approach. Her personal papers are full of her preparatory notes for each piece of music she worked on and are full of vast, complex equations. She broke sound down into numbers. Looking through her papers, it can seem that in her perception, music and maths were utterly indivisible.

After graduating, she had applied for a job at Decca but was told they did not employ women in their studios. She joined the U.N. to teach piano and maths to the children of important staff members, as well as at a local primary school. She finally joined the BBC after a stint at a music publisher, initially as a trainee assistant studio manager. Working on the programme *Record Review* her analytic approach to music quickly got her noticed. People would ask her to find a particular part of the record, which she could do by literally 'reading' the grooves of the vinyl record and putting the stylus down at the requested part[40]. Not an unknown skill but in that era and practised by an attractive young woman, it certainly raised eyebrows – in Derbyshire's own words *"[music critics] thought it was magic."*[41]

Most Radiophonic Workshop members arrived after working for a time as studio managers but Derbyshire jumped straight from trainee Assistant Studio Manager to the Workshop. As soon as she learned of the Workshop she volunteered for a placement there, which puzzled her managers who normally had to assign people against their will to fill such roles. The Workshop had a strange reputation within the BBC. The peculiar idea that it was unhealthy to work there any longer than a few months had persisted beyond Daphne Oram's day, and as a result Derbyshire's new role was only meant to be a temporary placement. However she had found her niche, and she resisted all attempts to return her to the world of studio management.

In 1962, Derbyshire's first piece of music for television was broadcast, for a documentary entitled *Time on Our Hands*. It examined the potential problems people would face in the future if technology became capable of doing all required work and left humanity with enormous amounts of leisure time. Sadly for twenty-first century workers, the premise proved less than prophetic, but Derbyshire's work was first rate, a beautiful mixture of melody and futurism. Her 1963 arrangement of "Get Out And Get Under" was created for *Family Car*, a programme about car maintenance, of all things. It was rejected by the producers as they feared people would think the car featured in the programme made the same sounds Derbyshire used in the theme tune. However, it demonstrated to Desmond Briscoe how ably she could work with other people's compositions and pointed the way to her best known single piece of work: the *Doctor Who* theme.

In fact, the Radiophonic Workshop was not Doctor Who producer Verity Lambert's first choice to arrange the theme to the new show. Initially she wanted French act Structures Sonores Lasry-Baschet. This quartet created strange, futuristic music through playing specially created sculptures. As Delia Derbyshire once commented of the unusual timbres they utilised:

"Their music sounded really electronic but in fact they were all acoustic instruments."[42]

However, Verity Lambert's boss, Sydney Newman, felt it would be cheaper and no less contemporary to get the Radiophonic Workshop to create the theme, recommending Ron Grainer for the task on the back of his work on *Giants of Steam*.

Ron Grainer [1922-1981]

There was another problem, though as Brian Hodgson recalls. "Ron Grainer had declared that he wasn't going to do any more theme tunes. Now the producers said they wanted something that sounded like Structures Sonores playing a Ron Grainer theme tune. Desmond knew Ron quite well and Ron had said he'd always wanted to do something specially for us, so Desmond said if you like I'll phone him up and see if he'll agree to do it. Desmond rang him there and then and he agreed to do a piece. He came in one day and scribbled the theme down on a torn off bit of manuscript paper. Delia actually wrote a lot of the links in it to make it work."[43]

Composer Grainer left for holiday assuming a band would collaborate with the Workshop for his piece and had consequently created music to be played by various musicians with some weird sound over the top. As Delia Derbyshire recalled "[o]n the score he'd written 'sweeps', 'swoops'... 'wind cloud', 'wind bubble.'"[44]

This full band composition proved no obstacle to Delia. She went to work with oscillators, then cutting and splicing tapes, speeding them up and slowing them down to achieve the right notes.

When he returned to the Workshop to hear the results, Grainer was very surprised. An appealing, and oft repeated, legend has it that, on hearing the amended tune, Grainer asked Derbyshire "Did I compose that?", to which she replied "most of it". Sadly, her friend and sometime collaborator Sonic Boom says she confessed this conversation never happened[45]. Even if not literally true, however, this apocryphal anecdote neatly illustrates how much Derbyshire contributed to the theme tune.

Another piece of received wisdom on the matter recounts that Grainer wanted Derbyshire to be given a co-writer's credit for her work on the *Who* theme, but persons unknown vetoed the idea. While most accounts simply refer to the BBC's preference that Workshop members not get individual credits for music, Derbyshire herself stated "...*we got a free Radio Times. The boss wouldn't let anybody have any sort of credit*"[46], referring to Desmond Briscoe.

In fact, the composers at the Workshop at the time weren't actually considered to be composers. They were originally paid as studio managers, albeit a specialised kind of studio manager. The standard BBC contract at the time gave the BBC the sole right to anything created by one of their employees, even if it were made away from BBC premises, assuming that it was relevant to radio or television. Since studio managers were receiving a regular salary, the BBC assumed that they had the right to claim any monies made via the Performing Rights Society (PRS), when Radiophonic music was played, or via the Mechanical-Copyright Protection Society (MCPS), when recordings were sold to the public. Only when the issue was brought to a head by John Baker was it realised that the BBC had, probably in ignorance, misunderstood the law: they were entitled, as a 'record producer' to collect the profit made via MCPS, but not the composer's profits via PRS. From that time forward the composers, now actually given their correct title, were able to receive PRS payments.

There's no doubt whatsoever that Delia Derbyshire's work on the *Doctor Who* theme formed part of the actual composition, as she built the music up with various embellishments. At the time, however, she couldn't be credited even as part-composer because the terms of her contract gave the credit to the BBC, along with Ron Grainer, who didn't work for the Corporation. Unfortunately, the BBC didn't give her any credit in hindsight either, nor any payments, presumably thinking that since she had left their employment it was no longer a problem. They no doubt also thought that any kind of acknowledgement would open the flood-gates to other retrospective PRS claims.

The musician Sonic Boom, who spent a great deal of time with Derbyshire towards the end of her life, noted that *"[i]t was one of things that bummed her out and stopped her making music"*[47]. Conversely, her colleague and close friend Brian Hodgson pointed out *"If Grainer had intended her to have her royalties then he should have declared her interest when he registered the piece. He had to register it himself and there was nothing to stop him, as he didn't work for the BBC."*[48]

The Workshop had originally been thought of mainly as a producer of unusual sound effects, but by now their output was becoming much more melodic. In such an environment, the rule regarding writing credits had become increasingly out-dated.

John Baker [1937-1997]

John Baker, who joined the Workshop in 1963, was the person who finally managed to force a change in the rules regarding composer credits. Baker's background was studying the piano and composition at the prestigious Royal Academy of Music. He had additionally played jazz since a young age and brought something very different to the Workshop.

Coming from such a musician-focused background, he was the first to push for individual authorship of pieces created at the Workshop and successfully applied to the PRS for it. Whilst the BBC still maintained the mechanical rights to work made in the Workshop, musical composers within the group were now recognised as just that and retained the intellectual copyright in their compositions.

Whilst Derbyshire's approach to melody and rhythm was a very mathematical one, Baker was an improviser and a skilled pianist. He brought a musician's touch to his work and while he did create abstract electronic recordings, he is best known for his catchy melodies set to intricate arrangements, utilising everyday sounds pitched into the right notes.

The classic example of this is the theme he devised for the popular radio show *Woman's Hour*, where he used the sound of someone blowing into a bottle and arranged it into a jaunty little theme with a ruler twang miraculously transformed into a bassline. It caused such fascination that he produced a short piece for the programme, explaining how he had created the theme.

Whilst many Workshop members found themselves forever associated with their work on *Doctor Who*, John Baker never worked on anything that made a lasting impression on the cultural memory of the public (though a piece he created for sci-fi anthology series *Out of the Unknown* found a second home on *Doctor Who* when it was re-used in the Patrick Troughton serial, 'The Macra Terror'), with the result that today his TV and radio themes are most commonly experienced purely as works of music with little media context attached. Perhaps because of this, he was the first member of the Workshop to be the subject of a major anthology, a two part CD compilation from Trunk Records, *The John Baker Tapes*.

Unfortunately, for all his talent and drive Baker had personal problems which began to affect his ability to work. He fell prey to depression and alcoholism. Baker took advantage of the Workshop's flexible working system (caused by the availability of the limited facilities), and began working more at night. He said it was to avoid Desmond Briscoe, but the suspicion was that he was drinking while working. His work began to suffer and he became less prolific and less accessible. Eventually, after doing all they could to help him, he was sacked by Briscoe in 1974 and never created any more music or performed in public again.

David Cain [born 1941]

David Cain was the next major composer to join the Workshop, in 1967. Like Delia Derbyshire, he had a mathematical background and started out as a studio manager, but he also had a strong interest in baroque and medieval music, leading Desmond Briscoe to jokingly label him *"Our only living medieval composer"*.

Like many at the Workshop, he did his fair share of radio jingles and other low visibility pieces, but he also landed some major dramatic composition jobs for BBC Radio. In his first year at the Workshop he did all of the incidental music for a large multi-part production of HG Wells' *The War of the Worlds*, and the next year he scored the BBC's prestigious radio adaptation of JRR Tolkien's *The Hobbit*. For this he created special sound effects with Dick Mills, and then composed the incidental music which was performed by David Munrow with the Early Music Consort. Cain's radiophonic work even crossed the planet – in 1967 his composition 'Crossbeat' was used by the Australian ABC network as the theme for a radio current affairs programme. The days of the Workshop being regarded merely as knob twiddlers who made only sound effects were definitely over.

Exemplifying this sea change, in 1968, a record was created to showcase the Workshop to other departments and provide music that could be re-used for any BBC productions. Entitled simply *BBC Radiophonic Music*, it consisted solely of music from Derbyshire, Baker and Cain. In 1970, when BBC Records was created, it was given a commercial release and - lacking a distinctive official title - it became known unofficially as "The Pink Album" because of its unusual front cover. It proved a popular album from its release, and was recently re-released in a deluxe re-mastered 180g vinyl edition, having previously been digitally re-mastered for CD with bonus tracks.

Cain left the Workshop in 1973, the same year he produced, directed, did special sound and composed the soundtrack for an adaption of Isaac Asimov's original *Foundation* trilogy. The series was repeated on BBC Radio in 2007, then made available for download, making it currently the only readily available adaptation of Foundation. Although some discussion is critical of the actual drama, the majority of its critics remain kind about the sound.[49] However, Cain's greatest contribution to musical history surely remains his BBC Schools LP *The Seasons*, which was rescued from obscurity (and high prices) by Trunk Records in 2012. *The Seasons* is a particularly prescient release that blends poetry praising the titular seasons with beautifully simple electronic melodies.

If Daphne Oram, Dick Mills and Desmond Briscoe had been the leading lights of the Workshop in the fifties, then for the sixties the torch was undoubtedly passed to Delia Derbyshire, Brian Hodgson, John Baker and David Cain. Theirs was a distinctive era before the advent of the synthesizer but no longer occupying a specialist niche as it had in the previous decade. A scan of the internet's discussion boards and comments sections clearly shows that for most fans, this was the golden age of the Radiophonic Workshop.

It is difficult to argue with such an estimation, but equally there remained much of value to come from the Workshop, and it is equally possible to view the nineteen seventies as the peak of the department's success.

Chapter Three – "Fag ends and Lollipops"

The 1970s saw a key development in music technology.

Electronic Music Studios (EMS) and Bob Moog had begun marketing synthesizers in the previous decade, and the Moog had appeared on late sixties albums by The Doors, Simon and Garfunkel and the Byrds, amongst others. Featured prominently at the Monterey Music Festival in 1967, Wendy Carlos finally brought the instrument into the public consciousness with the release of the triple Grammy Award winning *Switched-On Bach* in 1969. In the same year, Dick Hyman's Moog heavy jazz track 'The Minotaur' reached number 38 in the US music charts, and the Beatles adopted it for several tracks on *Abbey Road*.

The instrument the modern listener understands as a synthesizer only came into its own in the seventies, however. The development of miniaturised solid-state components added portability to the novel ability to create new and artificial sound instead of simply mimicking traditional instrumentation.

In 1970 the Minimoog was released by RA Moog Inc. A portable electronic synthesizer which was relatively affordable compared to the alternatives on the market, the Minimoog was cannily created with an eye to live performance, in order to capitalise on the growing mainstream interest in electronic sounds. As composer David Burden said of the Minimoog in 2005, at the time of its creator's death, it *"took the synthesizer out of the studio and put it into the concert hall"*[50].

Moog's rivals took note. 1972 saw EMS start producing their Sythi A, which for the first time offered a built in keyboard as standard. The same year, ARP released their best-selling Odyssey synth, another portable keyboard-based instrument. The synthesizer was no longer a cumbersome, fragile thing bound to a studio and controlled with dials. Nothing would ever be quite the same again. Daphne Oram's dream of an electronic instrument which created sounds unknown in nature was now a reality.

Time for a brief personal digression.

While I'm sure that the *Doctor Who* fans are still with us, some of the music aficionados may feel their enthusiasm draining somewhat at this point. Contemporary music journalism places enormous emphasis on the Workshop's sixties' output and is often scathingly derogatory towards what came afterwards. Simply put, we are no longer in the fashionable part of the book. Of course, it should go without saying that fashion is among the least appropriate ways to approach an art form like music, but even so, many still view it in such terms.

It may simply be that now that the synthesizer has become a commonplace musical instrument, it has been stripped of any mystique. For the listener born after 1970, the synth will seem as everyday as the guitar or the church organ. Its heavy use in cinema and television peaked in the eighties and almost entirely ceased the decade afterwards, however. Since then, the full orchestra has dominated movie theatres and anything with a heavily synth-based soundtrack automatically dates itself to a specific point in time.

The more complex and difficult analogue equipment used before the arrival of synthesizers, on the other hand, retains an air of rarity and novelty to the modern listener. It still sounds futuristic whereas the synthesizer has found itself in the popular perception to be something of a retro instrument. It is not, perhaps, entirely surprising that this is the case as the synth has become an affordable and accessible instrument for musicians in a way that large banks of oscillators never could be

Returning to *Doctor Who*, in 2007 I watched the classic, twentieth century series of the show with my American wife for the first time. She was hugely impressed by the 1960s episodes, with their unearthly analogue soundscapes which were like nothing she had ever heard before, but the later synth soundtracks made her cringe because to her they sounded so dated.

The old adage that "familiarity breeds contempt" very much applies here, and at the time of writing it takes a careful, mature listener to give this music the listening appreciation it deserves. Of course, the ever changing vagaries of fashion mean that anyone reading this book more than a few months after its publication may be left scratching their heads at this bizarre description of the synth! A sound considered dated at one point can swiftly be rehabilitated and regain its position as a contemporary musical element. This could well be the fate for synthesizer music.

There certainly seems to be a lot of good synthesizer music released in the last couple of years, especially from Europe's underground cassette labels. The soundtrack to the movie *Drive* follows a similar trend, by using old sounds in new ways, creating a more stripped down and moody approach to the instrument in high definition digital recording. A new generation of musicians is emerging who are too young to carry the old prejudices against the synthesizer. Its fall into obscurity as an instrument has been the key to its resurrection, and a critical reassessment of the Workshop's output from the seventies is now overdue.

In 1974 the German group Tangerine Dream moved to a more synth heavy sound with their fifth album *Phaedra*. The critics had been quite hostile towards their first four albums (although as they fit more neatly with the nebulous 'krautrock' genre, they are now better regarded by critics and lovers of experimental music, who often remain hostile to *Phaedra* and all successive albums). By the nineteen eighties Tangerine Dream were having a great deal of success producing soundtracks for Hollywood (while – ironically – the Radiophonic Workshop produced far superior work for the BBC, much of which is still commercially unreleased), but commercial success came at the price of critical praise and the band fell out of favour although they retained a loyal following. When the band's founder and sole constant member,

Edgar Frose died in 2015, the band were hailed as pioneers of synthesizer music in most of his obituaries. A better term might have been "popularisers" for they no more pioneered synthesizer music than The Beatles pioneered psychedelic music – they were just the ones who managed to sell it to the masses!

Remaining within the world of soundtracks, when it comes to the 70s and 80s, the Workshop's synth output is usually overlooked in favour of the likes of Goblin and John Carpenter, whose work has recently been reissued and reappraised by mainstream critics allowing them to dominate the discussion. However, they were scoring a very different type of media. As much as the BBC is considered to have a diverse output, bloody horror has never figured hugely among its output - the press would have had a field day if it did!

Thus, to even try and compare Carpenter's tense minimalism or Goblin's wild demonic sounds with the Workshop's output is pointless, the equivalent of trying to compare The Stooges or Iron Maiden with Oscar Peterson. The vast difference in genre and approach make such a comparison redundant and it is time that Workshop output from that era began to appear on the same lists.

In 1970, the Workshop took delivery of its first synth, the EMS VCS3, a "funky little unit"[51] with an angled wooden case. It was all knobs, dials, switches and a little joystick (a plug-in keyboard was available separately) - not a million miles away from the layout of *Doctor Who*'s TARDIS console, in fact. Although Bob Moog had approached the

Radiophonic Workshop in a bid to sell them his products, EMS had beaten him to the sale. The triumph of EMS over Moog was inevitable, in hindsight - they were far cheaper, they were British (and the British Broadcasting Corporation had to be seen to be supporting British innovation) and the EMS organisation were very close to Delia Derbyshire and Brian Hodgson. Hodgson had even started bringing his own VCS3 into the Workshop each day to help him with his work, an action which quickly became embarrassing for the BBC

It was something of a special relationship as Derbyshire and Hodgson had founded Unit Delta Plus in 1966 with Peter Zinovieff of EMS, whilst another EMS member, Tristram Cary, had provided soundtracks for the early Dalek stories on *Doctor Who*, during which time he had conferred a good deal with Brian Hodgson. Both Derbyshire and Hodgson knew the technology well, having been using it since it was a prototype and they vouched for it to Desmond Briscoe.

The VCS3 was also relatively portable compared to its peers and quickly established itself not just at the Workshop but among many of the more forward thinking bands of the day. Brian Eno used one in Roxy Music, Kraftwerk used one as did many others, including The Who, King Crimson, Pink Floyd (allegedly introduced to the VCS3 by Delia Derbyshire during a 1967 visit to the Workshop)[52], Gong, Hawkwind, The Groundhogs and many more.

The next acquisition was an EMS Sythi 100, an enormous beast of an instrument, the biggest voltage-controlled synthesizer in the world. Christened "The Delaware" after the road the studios were on, it was enormously complicated, with banks of dials and a frustrating habit of slipping out of tune when the temperature changed, but crucially it offered a host of new possibilities and just as many new challenges. One person who seemed to take more enthusiastically to these challenges was the newest member of the Workshop, Malcolm Clarke [1943-2003].

Clarke is said to have stirred things up at the Workshop. Unlike his colleagues, he took the view that Radiophonic Music was fine art. His first big break was taking over from *Doctor Who*'s regular composer Dudley Simpson to create the sound track (not the special sound) for the 1972 serial 'The Sea Devils'. Composed exclusively on the EMS Synthi 100, the results remain controversial to this day.

His score for it is brutal, relentless, intense and discordant. While attitudes towards electronic music have softened considerably since 1972, it still retains the power to shock - and to alienate! Look up 'The Sea Devils' on the internet, and it can be fascinating just how much the soundtrack continues to polarise opinion, with many finding it offensively noisy. One person shocked by it was series' producer, Barry Letts, who ordered that cuts be made[53], and as a consequence the Radiophonic Workshop was not asked to provide a soundtrack for *Doctor Who* again until 1980, although they continued to provide special sound for the show.

Ray White, who worked alongside him for many years recalls

"*Malcolm Clarke was definitely a 'one off', certainly a 'ladies' man' and one who appreciated the finer things in life, especially the avant-garde or the abstract, making his work on the programme* Salvador Dali and his Witnesses, *broadcast in 1980, a very special project for him. He also liked seeing the world through the eyes of a child, as demonstrated by his track 'Bath Time', and often employed low-cost synthesisers and other electronic devices to create crude and often 'challenging' sounds. His view that electronic music should be 'high art' isn't 'controversial', as some might say, but is similarly challenging. He was, I suppose, similar to Daphne Oram in his approach to music, preferring to create pure forms of sound, rather than just something as an accompaniment to ready-made visuals. I remember that he had this grand idea that one day there would be an visual equivalent in the BBC to the Workshop, and that composers would then be able to work on the whole multimedia experience, rather than with sound alone.*

'Others at the Workshop often mocked him, in a kindly manner, about his high aspirations. I do remember on one occasion, I think it may have been his birthday, when a die-cast aluminium box was sneakily 'installed' in his studio, appropriately labelled 'FART BOX', which gave all concerned, including Malcolm, a great deal of amusement. He could be very awkward at times, but it's the nature of a true artist to be challenging."[54]

After nine years of creating the sounds for *Doctor Who*, Brian Hodgson left the Workshop in 1972 and Dick Mills took over the job of providing "special sound" for the show, a role he maintained until its cancellation in 1989.

Mills' evolving role was reflective of the changes at the Workshop. Previously there had been composers to make sounds, and engineers to provide technical support, as well as develop and maintain the equipment. Mills had joined not as a studio manager but as a technical operator, responsible for adjusting or lining-up tape machines, playing in cues and editing tapes. Mills had proven himself a master at this - assisting Delia Derbyshire in creating the *Doctor Who* theme for example - that he ended up being asked to put those skills to more autonomous creative purposes. Such credit seemed to arrive a little retrospectively, with Mills already having had a hand in many of the best known pieces of work from the Workshop's history (he was, after all, the man who created the sound of Major Bloodnok's stomach for *The Goon Show* in 1959). His sly shift to composer led to him creating pieces of music for TV and radio alongside his special sound duties for *Doctor Who*.

The next addition to the group was Paddy Kingsland in 1970. He came to the Workshop after working as a studio manager at Radio 1 (the BBC's pop music radio station). He started out creating indents and themes for TV and radio, proving himself a dab hand with catchy melodies, much like John Baker. The same year, Richard Yeomen-Clarke joined. He had gone straight from school to the BBC working as a technical operator at first before switching to being a recording engineer at the Experimental Stereo Unit. His familiarity with stereo lead to his elevation to the role of Studio Manager for the music department, where he worked with the likes of Stockhausen.

With such a background he was a neat fit for The Radiophonic Workshop, creating the special sound for *Blakes 7* and working as technical coordinator for the implementation of the new synthesizers. Wednesday 19th May 1971 also saw a prestigious event at the Royal Albert Hall billed as "Radiophonic Workshop in Concert", with the terribly British subtitle, 'Ingenious Electric Entertainment'[55]. A celebration of the 100th anniversary of the Institute of Electrical engineers, Brian Hodgson directed the show, Desmond Briscoe devised and presented it and EMS loaned the synths, while the programme gave prominence to the premiere of a new piece by Delia Derbyshire, *IEE 100*, "*especially composed for the occasion.*[56]"

Though *IIE 100* has never been released in full, Desmond Briscoe has described the piece in detail in *The First 25 Years*:

"*Taking the initial letters IEE, Delia composed music from their mathematical correspondences and from morse code: introducing elements of the development of electricity in communication from the earliest telephone to the Americans landing on the moon. There was the voice of Mr Gladstone congratulating Mr Edison on inventing the phonograph: the opening and closing down of Savoy Hill with Lord Reith's voice: and Neil Armstrong speaking as he stepped onto the surface of the moon. The powerful punch of Delia's rocket take-off threatened the very fabric of the Festival Hall."*[57]

However, the night before the concert she still wasn't satisfied with the seven minute piece and was still working on it. Sensing her volatile mood, Hodgson had Richard Yeomen-Clarke, who was assisting Delia, to secretly make a copy of the tape and give it to him. When he came in the next morning, Derbyshire was in tears and told him she had destroyed the tape in frustration because it was not working. Hodgson knew her only too well and the piece was played out to the Royal audience, much to Derbyshire's dismay[58].

Part of what had made Delia Derbyshire and John Baker's work so special was their willingness to labour for hours through the night, painstakingly cutting tapes and editing. With the newly emergent technology making such heroic efforts redundant, both composers seemed to lose their confidence and creative drives. Work was also expected to be completed far more quickly as the pace of life in general intensified. The arrival of a new generation who were completely at home with such methods can only have added to their sense of alienation. Back in the '60s Derbyshire and Baker would both spend weeks on a single project but with the new technology around, this was no longer necessary or even allowed. As obsessive perfectionists, the stricter deadlines were anathema to their whole way of working.

Delia Derbyshire left the Workshop in 1972. Asked why in 2000 all she could say was "I still haven't worked out why I left – self-preservation I think.[59]"

A plan had been hatched for the Workshop to release a second commercial record with one half recorded by John Baker and the other half by Paddy Kingsland. Unfortunately, Baker was by now becoming erratic and unreliable, and a combination of his increased drinking and a reluctance to embrace the new synthesizer technology was causing problems. The album that came out, 1973's *Fourth Dimension*, while credited to the BBC Radiophonic Workshop was all the work of Kingsland. In the end, John Baker did not leave until 1974, but his leaving, when it came, was not voluntary, as he was fired and never made music professionally again.

As Derbyshire was leaving, a new face was joining - Roger Limb. Although his previous role at the BBC had been as a TV announcer, before that he had been (like everyone else, it seems!) a studio manager. He had learnt piano as a child before taking on the double bass at age fifteen, then studying music as both a conductor and composer. After graduating, he joined a touring jazz band and still plays jazz to the present day, often playing prestigious venues like Ronnie Scott's.

Limb was friends with Paddy Kingsland, whose suggestion it was that he join. He initially did a three month attachment and then joined permanently in 1974. He was followed soon after by Glynis Jones. Slightly before that, in 1973, David Cain had left, having obtained (like Daphne Oram before him) a Gulbenkian Grant[60].

1975 saw the release of a new compilation, this time simply entitled *The Radiophonic Workshop*, featuring all current members of the Workshop from John Baker and Dick Mills right up to Glynis Jones and Roger Limb. Consisting almost entirely of specially written new material, it presented the Workshop in stereo for the first time ever. Freed from the constraints of composing for television, the results were wildly contrasting, from tasteful, subtle minimalism from Dick Mills right up to a rowdy, rambunctious electronic waltz from Malcolm Clarke.

    Although it came out in 1975, the album was recorded too late to include Peter Howell, who joined the Workshop in 1974, having previously been a (guess what?) studio manager. His background included spells playing in psychedelic folk groups such as Ithaca, Friends and Agincourt but, most importantly, he had experience of soundtrack work having created the score for 1969 hippy road movie *Tomorrow Comes Someday* with his usual writing partner John Ferdinando.

In 1975, the Workshop was asked to create some extra material for the incidental music for "Revenge of the Cybermen", the final story from Tom Baker's first year as the Doctor. Composer Carey Blyton [1932-2002] had created a wonderful but unusual score for the serial utilising medieval wind instruments and producer Philip Hinchcliffe turned to the Workshop to enhance it a little. Peter Howell was the perfect choice with his background in psychedelic folk giving him a considerable understanding of what Blyton was doing. His synthesizer work fuses with Blyton's score in a very natural, sympathetic, and discreet way, whilst the addition of futuristic sounds made the soundtrack far more apt for a serial set in space thousands of years from now.

The following year saw Glynis Jones overseeing the album *Out Of This World* for the BBC's sound effects series. Drawing from the Radiophonic Workshop's archives, it collected lots of short pieces together for the first time. A letter from Jones to Delia Derbyshire in March of that year survives in the latter's archives and gives an interesting insight into the process. In the very brief letter, Jones informs Derbyshire of the album and which of her pieces are being used, as well as noting their new names so she could inform the Performing Rights Society. The idea that everyone's existing work was being renamed to fit the theme of the compilation suggests that titles given to music created at the Workshop were a bit more fluid than in other forms of music.

Elizabeth Parker, a graduate in Music and Fine Arts at the University of East Anglia, who had completed a postgraduate course on electronic music, joined the Workshop in 1976. During her postgrad course she studied tape manipulation, sound balanced orchestras and received tutorship from EMS co-founder, Tristram Cary. She went straight into the BBC as a Programme Operations Assistant, primarily doing sound balancing. This position involved ensuring that the volume of broadcasts were consistent and did not force the viewer or listener to adjust their volume dials in irritation.

Parker first joined on a three month trial period whilst Dick Mills was on holiday over the summer. As her audition, she had to send in a demonstration tape of sound effects for a radio production of *The Frog Prince*. Her first official task was special sound for the *Doctor Who* serial 'The Stones of Blood', which meant using tape manipulation to create the convincing sound of heavy stones moving around - and killing people. Though she left the Workshop once her placement was over, she returned later when Richard Yeoman-Clark left and took over his job of providing sound effects for popular BBC1 space serial, *Blakes 7*, starting with the second series.

Parker recalls "It was a real baptism of fire. My goodness, it was hard with deadlines and getting the equipment to work. A lot of tape loops and tape manipulation, the stuff everyone finds so fascinating now. I started doing a lot of background sounds, Servalan's bedroom had a nice spacey background. It was a good way in.[61]"

1978 also saw the Workshop put out two different releases for BBC Records. They contributed another compilation for the sound effects series, this time dedicated exclusively to *Doctor Who*, collecting Brian Hodgson and Dick Mills' special sounds.

The other release was a little more surprising, an artist album for Peter Howell, called *Through A Glass Darkly* and almost entirely containing new material. Clearly BBC Records were as keen to make use of the Workshop's services as the TV and Radio producers before them.

In 1979 the Workshop celebrated its twenty-first anniversary. To celebrate, a first ever retrospective compilation was issued, called simply *21*. Compiled by Brian Hodgson and Roger Limb, side one was in mono and focussed on the late fifties and sixties era of the Workshop, with many classic moments from Delia Derbyshire in particular. The original *Doctor Who* theme makes its first appearance on a Radiophonic Workshop album here and Maddalena Faggandini's original version of "Time Beat" is presented here in its original, pre-George Martin version. Intriguingly, Desmond Briscoe takes all the credit for the piece "Outside", a study in paranoid alienation. However, when it saw release on the CD *Retrospective* compilation it was co-credited to Maddalena Fagandini.

Side two was dedicated to the Workshop's current line-up, to synthesizers and in stereo. It's not quite a thorough chronology, however, as side one has nothing later than 1966 while side two has nothing earlier than 1973. The second side sees not just a shift in sound but in mood. The earlier material created through tape manipulation and studio trickery is overwhelmingly dark and cold. When you turn over to side two, there is a sudden overwhelming sense of optimism and utopian dreams. The synths are used to create fanfares, soothing moods and more welcoming alien landscapes than those invoked on the first side. Its tactile nature seems to lend it a warmer feel.

However, whilst the Workshop was doing well for new blood, it was not doing quite so well for new equipment. Brian Hodgson recalls:

"The Radiophonic Workshop never had a budget apart from the £2,000 it got when it started. It relied on what I called 'fag ends and lollipops'. Fag ends were bits of money left over from others peoples schemes, like if they built a new studio and there was £400 left over then we would get that. Lollipops were whenever Desmond got desperately uptight and started whining, they'd give him something to shut him up. They bought this massive new desk for one of the new studios but it wasn't needed so it ended up with us. The last thing we wanted was a massive £30,000 desk when the rest of the place was running on bits of twisted wire and sellotape[62]."

With Desmond Briscoe wanting to cut down on his workload as he approached retirement, a position was created as his assistant, with additional responsibility as a full time organiser of the Workshop. The job went to Brian Hodgson, returning after a five year absence from the Workshop:

"Delia was asked to apply, I was and other Workshop members were invited to apply. I was in a good position because, quite frankly, I didn't give a fuck whether I got it or not so I could be quite bold. I said if I if I do come back I want to make lots and lots of changes, especially to how the place is equipped. They took that onboard.

"I'd been doing experimental work with Ken Gale of Gale Electronics and had gotten a polyphonic keyboard and higher quality filters, oscillators. When I got back and saw the Delaware which was 1972 technology but by then it was like an antique and it was the best thing they had, everyone had to take turns sharing it. You could only have a studio for so many hours. It was a bloody shambles[63]."

Clearly something had to change at the Workshop, and Brian Hodgson was the man to make it happen.

Chapter Four: 'It was just the Pet Shop Boys and myself'

As the new organiser of the Workshop, Brian Hodgson was desperate to upgrade the department's increasingly outdated equipment. Before he could make any concrete decisions, however, a sizeable budget needed to be agreed.

"So I burnt the ear of John Dutot (who was the new head of resources for radio). I said it's ridiculous, we're doing all this work for television and we're equipped in the 1950s. So he spoke to the director of resources, I showed him round and did my bolshie whinge. He asked me to produce a report on what I want to do. He accepted that report and gave me £100,000 a year[64]."

Hodgson's plan was to use the budget to upgrade a studio a year. This eventually did lead to the Workshop gaining a reputation for, if not always state of the art, usually up to date equipment. By 1978, writers such as Douglas Adams were keen to use the Workshop for their radio plays, for instance, because they had a sixteen track machine[65] where others did not.

However, having the money to create such studios was not sufficient in itself. Hodgson needed people with the right skills too.

Ray White [born 1952] had joined the BBC as a maintenance engineer in 1973, soon after graduating in electrical engineering from Portsmouth Polytechnic.

White had first been attached to the Workshop in the mid-seventies, and described the technical conditions as *"dreadful"* with the majority of the equipment not having been updated since the nineteen sixties, and the available workspace at Maida Vale largely comprised of 'converted offices' in a series of rooms which were ranged along the corridor of the Maida Vale Studios. The combination of antiquated machinery and studio space *'developed piecemeal'* in White's own words, cannot help but indicate an under-funded and increasingly neglected organisation.

When long term engineer Dave Young retired there was a rapid succession of engineers coming and going before Ray White joined permanently as Senior Engineer in 1979 (before that White had done a second placement at the Workshop). One particularly interesting practice he noted on his first visit was that, in his office, Desmond Briscoe was able to listen in to any of the Workshop's studios! Something that White does not believe was popular with the composers, for obvious reasons, and that ended once Briscoe retired[66].

As Brian Hodgson recalls, there appears to have been a fight for White between the Workshop and Technical Services:

"We'd had a series of dimwit engineers and suddenly Ray White was on the horizon and the engineering people were unhappy about him being got by the Workshop but I got him back and had him spearheading the engineering side. We managed to redo a studio every year, bring it up to date[67]*."*

White himself recollects that Technical Services even went as far as to imply to the Workshop that he did not want to join them, leading to another engineer being appointed after White's second placement, and briefly delaying White's permanent appointment. In the end, Desmond Briscoe was not taking any chances and before doing the official interview in the full gaze of the BBC, White was summoned to Briscoe's office for a practise interview to make sure he said all the right things on the record.

Another Ray, Ray Riley (like White, a former maintenance engineer), also joined the Workshop at around the same time, and the two Rays set out updating the studios. Given the condition they were in, this was an enormous undertaking that would take up most of their time at the Workshop.

British culture in the past often divided the world of the artist from that of the engineer, and this was certainly the case in the BBC during the time of the Workshop. The engineer was sometimes perceived as the 'person in the overalls with a large spanner', whilst the artist was considered to be more cultured or of a higher class. Those in the creative echelons were often graduates from Cambridge and other, similarly renowned, seats of learning, but those in engineering came from technical colleges and polytechnics. This didn't prevent people of humble origins climbing to very high positions within the BBC, but there was still a strong division between the 'operational' staff of radio and television and the 'engineering' departments.

There were two distinct camps in the Workshop, then - the artistic composers and the practical engineers. Even in terms of reporting, the composers were answerable to Brian Hodgson and Desmond Briscoe, while the engineers were answerable to technical managers at Broadcasting House. Ray White recalls that:

"towards the end of each mid-monthly meeting Desmond would often 'dismiss' the engineers whilst he and the composers would go on to talk about higher things as Desmond seemed to think the engineers did not know about art[68]!"

Even so, White recalls the Workshop feeling not like a segregated workplace, but as a tight and cohesive unit, with all staff, in whatever role, keen to work for the best of the department as a whole. Jonathan Gibbs, for example, was a Cambridge graduate who worked alongside White on the Syncwriter project (see below), whilst White often worked with Peter Howell on the development of studio systems. Perhaps most telling in this respect is Dick Mills' remark that *"everyone who works here is here for two reasons: they wanted to come, and Desmond Briscoe chose them to stay"*[69]

In spite of the improvements brought about by Brian Hodgson, Paddy Kingsland left the Workshop in 1981 to set up his own studio just as Hodgson's technological renewals were beginning to take effect. Elizabeth Parker recalls:

"Suddenly I seemed to have quite a lot of equipment. Around 1981 I had a PPG, I think it was just the Pet Shop Boys and myself who had one, a sampler machine. You could put the sound into a computer and manipulate it on the screen instead of with a razor blade.

"The pressures got a lot harder because it was quicker to make the music, people expected it much more quickly and it was running in parallel with all the technical stuff going on with television where everyone could work quicker. You didn't have the luxuries that they had had in the sixties to take two weeks to make twenty seconds of sound."[70]

1983 was the twenty-fifth anniversary of the Radiophonic Workshop and, to celebrate, BBC Books commissioned journalist Roy Curtis-Bramwell to write a book about the history of the Workshop with the assistance of Desmond Briscoe.

The book, subtitled *The First 25 Years*, was the first proper account of the Workshop to see print. Prior to its publication, the Workshop had been the subject of brief, superficial newspaper articles, but they tended to be in non-musical publications, as the form of electronica the Workshop championed was still often anathema to the British musical press. Publication of the *25 Years* book, however, provided a sense of legitimacy for the department. In fact, it is a very good book, factual without being overly technically intimidating to the layman, with plenty of fascinating photos, and an easy and quite witty writing style, as one would expect from a professional journalist like Curtis-Bramwell.

However, Daphne Oram was furious.

So what had happened? Curtis-Bramwell had visited Oram at her home on August 24th the previous year and the next day had written to her thanking her for her hospitality and assuring her he would be in touch. On December 3rd, Oram wrote a letter to Curtis-Bramwell, stating her concern that the book was reaching proof stage and she had still not had the chance to fact check the parts of the book that related to her. On her own copy of the letter, Oram noted "D BRISCOE replied by telephone 7th Dec – he will send galley proofs. No reply from Roy Curtis Bramwell"[71]

Oram finally received a letter from Desmond Briscoe, dated January 14th:

Dear Daphne,

As promised, and in great haste, for the galley proofs have only just arrived (they were promised last Friday!) I enclose photocopies of the pages where your name appears. As the proofs have to be back with the editor on Monday (17th January) I would be most grateful if you could check this for factual accuracy and let me have them back by return post – I enclose a stamped addressed envelope to save you time and trouble.

As I explained to you on the phone, Roy's original text has been very heavily edited and at a very hurried glance during lunch (I'm in the studio producing a programme at present!) these seem to be the relevant mentions, but obviously if I discover anything else I will get in touch by phone

Yours sincerely

Desmond Briscoe
Head of Radiophonic Workshop

Daphne's own notes on the letter state that she returned amendments that night. The next day, another letter arrived:

Dear Daphne

 More haste less speed! I have found the nice reference to Amphitryon 38 *which I am sure you would like to see and I also enclose a copy of the whole of Chapter 2, which deals with the pre-Workshop time and typically manages to do so without mentioning either of us!*

There is nothing we can do about this at this stage, so please don't bother to rush around trying to get this back to me by Monday.

Yours sincerely

Desmond Briscoe
Head of Radiophonic Workshop.

Among the things Oram wanted changed was the fact that the book contained details on where she lived and advertised the fact that she had a recording studio at home. She lived on her own and was worried this might attract burglars, higher rates from the local authority, and unwanted correspondence. She also wanted the fact that she spent nine to ten years trying to get the BBC to set up an electronic studio to be mentioned in the book.

She pointed out that *Amphitryon 38* was not the first programme to be worked on at the Workshop, because the Workshop had not actually opened at that point. She also drew attention to the fact that Jeremy Sandford and Humphrey Searle were not credited for their pre-Workshop Radiophonic work at the BBC.

On the 17th of January 1983, Oram wrote to the Managing Director of BBC Radio, Richard Francis, to complain about the book. She asked them to delay publishing and firmly blamed Desmond Briscoe for editing her out of the picture and included her own personal account of her involvement in the Workshop and her contributions. She also took great offence at what had been written about her, retorting:

"On Nov 1st 1958, I handed in my resignation as, by that time, I could see that the Workshop was going to handle very little music – only extended sound effects as required by such producers as Douglas Cleverdon and Donald McWhinnie. I wished to continue to compose. I was not, as suggested in the galley proof, wanting to get in on the act after visiting Brussels – I had been composing such music

since 1949, some 3 years before Cologne started their studio! I was just wanted to develop the techniques quietly for some years before presently my music to the public. To do this I did not set up a studio "on a ludicrous sealing wax and string basis" as the galley proofs state – if I had done so I would have been unlikely to be invited, in 1961, to appear and present my music at the Edinburgh Festival, nor would I have received a Gulbenkian Grant in 1962"

The response from Francis was dated March 18th and defended the book and Desmond Briscoe. He stated that *"[t]he book is concerned primarily with what happened after 1958 and since that time more than sixty staff have been attached to the Workshop, many of them for longer periods than you yourself. I think it quite logical that the accounts of other people should also be taken into consideration"* but did at least go on to allow that *"... the Workshop owes much to your own skill and great enthusiasm in those early days. I do hope you will accept the enclosed invitation to the celebrations on 31st March*[72]*."*

Whatever the rights and wrongs (Oram alleged to Richard Francis that Briscoe had not joined the Workshop until 1962, Francis replying that records showed him as starting there in 1958), it was a sad state of affairs that one of the leading lights of the early days of Radiophonics now felt so betrayed. The issues she had with the original proof do not, for the most part, appear in the finished book, so it seems that while no fault was acknowledged by the BBC publically, they quietly complied with all her requests.

Whether due to her complaints or not, Daphne Oram receives only a few fleeting mentions in the final text. She is briefly described as "a prime mover in the cause" of getting an electronic music studio at the BBC in the section regarding the period before the formation of the Workshop and is next referred to as "the senior founder member" upon her departure. The reference to her "ludicrous sealing wax and string" set up is excised along with the implication that she was only inspired to take up electronic music after visiting the 1958 *Journées Internationales de Musique Expérimentale* in Brussels and even points out that she had already been working on electronic music for eight years before that event. It is also quite complimentary about her career after the Workshop, although these parts seem to be taken almost word for word from her correspondence with the BBC over the book.

The rift between Desmond Briscoe and Daphne Oram is perhaps best ascribed to the fact that they were two such different people, as Ray White, who worked for Desmond Briscoe for many years, describes.

"Desmond was very clever at ascribing things to himself, often saying 'I thought of that', no doubt because the survival of the Workshop had been somewhat tenuous in the early days and he needed every possible thing to cling to. Daphne Oram, thwarted in her desire to create a true electronic music studio at the BBC, clearly couldn't see beyond her own ambitions: at the time of formation the Workshop was expressly designed not to work in Music for

fear of upsetting the musical establishment in the Corporation.

"Desmond saw the long-term view and knew how to survive: he complied with the requirements of BBC management and connived continuously to obtain more resources and work for the department. Daphne Oram may well have been the greater artist, but she could not have ensured the Workshop's continuation. Indeed, if she had been running it, it would have closed much earlier. Desmond was, without doubt, a superb manager, one who could get the very best out of all the members of his team."

1983 was not all about books and anniversaries, though. It was also the year composer Jonathan Gibbs joined the Workshop, although his biggest project was not in composition but in creating a bespoke piece of software to help the composers cue their music to the film rushes they were sent. It was one of the most ambitious technical projects of the Workshop's history and resulted in a programme for the BBC micro-computer called Syncwriter.

Syncwriter enabled the composer to plot out their music in time with the video tape. It helped composers get a greater sense of timing, allowing them to pinpoint cues in the video at exact times and compose accordingly so that their finished work could simply be synchronised to the video tape. Syncrwrite made such an impression that Gibb dedicated a lot of time at the Workshop refining and updating the programme, even providing further support after he left the department.

When Desmond Briscoe retired at the end of 1983 and Brian Hodgson took over his role, he opted for newcomer Gibbs to be his assistant. By now Hodgson had managed drastically to increase the already much improved budget and not only were all seven studios fully refurbished, but they were constantly being updated so that all of them contained the very latest in synth and computer technology. After careful consideration and research, Gibbs and Hodgson decided upon the Macintosh computer as most suitable to their needs, and bought thirteen of them. The Macintosh was from now on an integral part of the Workshop, so much so that Brian Hodgson's fiftieth birthday cake was made in the shape of one.

Gibbs also found time to provide soundtracks for *Doctor Who*, working on some of Peter Davison's second series and Colin Baker's first. However, the demands of *Doctor Who* were taking their strain on the Radiophonic Workshop. Although he had left the Workshop, Paddy Kingsland continued to be commissioned on a freelance basis to provide music for the show. However, the series' producer, John Nathan Turner, was interested in working with other composers and the Workshop were equally interested in freeing up more time for other projects.

For one serial in 1985, 'The Mark Of The Rani', Brian Hodgson persuaded Nathan Turner to entrust the music to his old Electrophon and Wavemaker partner, John Lewis. Unfortunately, Lewis had completed the music for episode one and had only just begun on series two when he became too ill to continue. At this late stage, Brian Hodgson invited Jonathan Gibbs to begin the project all over again, whilst John Lewis sadly passed away from an AIDS-related illness. For the DVD release of the serial, archivist Mark Ayres restored the original soundtrack giving viewers the option to watch the episode with either the John Lewis soundtrack or the Jonathan Gibbs's version. After that, the Workshop created the soundtrack for one more *Doctor Who* serial in 1986, and then never again.

With the departure of Johnathan Gibbs in 1986, Richard Attree became the final composer permanently to join the Workshop (although Steve Marshall joined the Workshop for three months in 1988, covering for Malcolm Clarke while he was off sick). Attree's initial commissions were mostly for BBC Schools, although in 1995 he did get the job of creating the terrifying theme music to the BBC adaption of popular children's book *The Demon Headmaster*, an opportunity he seized with glee, creating something more fitting for a horror film soundtrack than a children's TV drama.

Attree was the only person to join the Workshop as a composer who had not previously been a BBC employee, as Brian Hodgson felt it was important to advertise the role externally to reflect that with new changes in home computer technology had made the need for full prior BBC studio training unnecessary. While with the Workshop, Attree won Sony awards - for "Most Creative Use of Radio" for "Peace on Earth" and "The Dream" - although these works seem to be forgotten and

Attree himself remains an obscure figure in the history of the Workshop.

Obviously, in retrospect, he joined the department at exactly the wrong time. 1986 was the year that *Doctor Who* commissioned a new theme tune to replace Peter Howell's - only not from the Radiophonic Workshop, but from an outside composer. With the incidental music already outsourced, the Workshop's sole contribution to a series which had in many ways defined them was to provide special sound.

This was the start of a sequence of events that would cause a severe decline in the fortunes of the Workshop and, eventually, its closure.

Chapter Five – "Shall I give you the key then?"

The end of the BBC Radiophonic Workshop came about through a mixture of politics and technology.

As a starting point, the BBC had long-since incurred the wrath of Prime Minister Margaret Thatcher and her government. Thatcher, an economic neo-liberal, believed the Corporation's very basis for existence was indefensible, both economically - with the license fee a state handout which should be scrapped - and morally - as she accused the BBC as a whole of being out of step with contemporary standards of decency and taste. In the recent past, the left-leaning Labour government of James Callaghan had considered making the BBC a genuine state broadcaster, by removing the license fee and replacing it with direct government funding, but Thatcher's preference was to force the Corporation to replace the license fee with advertising (matching the funding model for the existing independent television channels), if she could not bring it to heel.

The primary reason for this animosity, however, was not ideological or moral; instead, it was driven by a desire to punish an organisation which, Conservatives believed, was, at best, overly impartial and, at worst, openly antagonistic towards the government. Particular areas of contention included Northern Ireland (the BBC was criticised, for instance, for describing Bloody Sunday, the slaughter of 14 Irish Catholics by the Army in January 1972, as a 'massacre' and not a 'shooting') and the Falklands War (in her study of the BBC in the period, *Pinkoes and Traitors*, Jean Seaton recalls that Thatcher viewed the BBC as traitors for refusing to describe British troops in the conflict as 'our boys' and wished to forcefully take over the Corporation in order to guarantee positive reporting of government policies and initiatives, including those related to the Falklands)[73].

Conservatives complained about BBC bias in election coverage, and protested interviews with and documentaries about suspected terrorists and political opponents. Later in the decade, Party chairman Norman Tebbit led a campaign against the BBC's coverage of the 1986 American bombing of Libya, claiming it to be anti-American. When another documentary alleged links between Conservative MPs and various far right groups, two MPs successfully sued the BBC for libel. That the government and the BBC were at war was undeniable. The only question was who would emerge victorious and what would be lost in the process.

In the midst of these disagreements and political jockeying, the Chairman of the BBC's board, Stuart Young, unexpectedly died of cancer in his early fifties. Initially appointed by the government Young had proven to be a disappointment to Thatcher who viewed him as having "gone native" when he began retreated from an early pro-advertising stance and defended the TV license instead. Determined to take no risks with his replacement,

Thatcher appointed Marmaduke Hussey, who had close connections to the Conservative party and the right-wing of the UK media, as Young's successor.

It was unfortunate (or perhaps inevitable) that, soon afterwards, the BBC showed a series of TV and radio documentaries which the government believed breached national security. The result was the police raiding the TV production *Secret Society*, which lead to BBC journalists going on strike in protest. Soon afterwards, the government banned the radio documentary series *My Country Right or Wrong* and Hussey forced the Director-General, Alasdair Milne, to resign.

Milne was replaced with former accountant Michael Checkland and his deputy John Birt. Thatcher wrote that this was "an improvement in every respect" and the clashes between the BBC and her government ended as the Corporation buckled. Five years later, Checkland moved on and his deputy, Birt, took over. Birt was determined to run the BBC along the lines of a highly efficient business, a move that created a good deal of hostility within the BBC but which perfectly fitted the Conservatives free market policies. He introduced radical changes in a bid to cut costs, regardless of the impact on quality, the most notorious of which was Producer Choice

Unveiled in November 1991 and in full effect by 1993, Producer Choice sounded a death knell for the Radiophonic Workshop. Whilst previously the BBC had operated as a self-sufficient production entity, the new Producer Choice allowed programme makers to commission services from outside the BBC. This naturally led to the creation of an internal market, in which all BBC departments, including the Radiophonic Workshop, were placed in the invidious position of having to charge BBC producers for their services and to compete financially with external businesses, with quality very much of secondary importance. In the words of one commentator, *"with the introduction of Producer Choice, BBC management embraced the monopoly of neoliberal economic themes such as competition, consumer sovereignty and entrepreneurialism."*[74] In other words, exactly the same cut-throat, free market approach that the Conservative party so enthusiastically espoused.

The results were devastating to many of the BBC's in house departments. Elizabeth Parker recalls,

"We had to make our department pay so to make it work we had to charge ridiculous amounts of money. We would have to charge £5,000 for something someone would do for £1,000. It got absurd, we were having to make £60,000 a month to keep the workshop going. John Birt has a lot to answer for. There was no way we were ever going to make enough money to make it work[75]*"*

Birt remains a controversial figure to this day. A Labour supporter (he later worked as an advisor to Tony Blair) who eagerly embraced Thatcherite free market policy, he was, for some, the man saved the BBC from an excess of union power and launched it into the digital age.

For the majority of those who worked at the Corporation, however, he will always be remembered as the man who ruined the BBC and remorselessly destroyed departments, relying on management consultants, focus groups and accountants, rather than the creatives who had made the BBC the best loved and most well-known broadcaster in the world. By his own estimation, ten thousand people either resigned from the BBC or were made redundant during his years as Director General, as he attempted to outstrip Thatcher in the application of the political ideology which bore her name. Even now Birt's name comes up in most discussions on the future direction of the BBC, and Birtian, as a generally pejorative adjective, has entered the English language.

Perhaps if the BBC had not antagonised the government, Birt's changes might have been delayed, but they were probably inevitable at some point, given the Conservative's decade and a half in power, and Thatcher's ideological preference for self-sufficiency over state or public funding. Nobody is immune to the forces of change and it's generally agreed that there was a need for *some* modernisation at the BBC, but the result of Birt's reforms meant the death of a great many valuable institutions within the Corporation, including the Radiophonic Workshop.

However, Birt was not the only sweeping force of change with which the Workshop had to contend. By 1993, home computer technology had come in leaps and bounds. Both Apple Macintoshes and PCs came supplied with far more accessible and user-friendly operating systems and increasing demand was slowly driving down the costs. The new MIDI technology that the Workshop was so keen to take advantage of was also available to the public and whilst by no means cheap, it was possible to create a home electronic studio for little more money than it would cost for a new family car.

Although the first MIDI compatible synth came out in 1982, it had been a slow and steady rise at best, but by 1993 the concept of the home electronic music studio was now commonplace, as the dance music boom of the time proved. People were having top ten hits with music they had created in their bedrooms.

Suddenly the Radiophonic Workshop had literally hundreds of competitors in the UK alone. Many of these competitors were ready to drastically undercut the Workshop on price. Producer Choice was not a sudden cut but a slow death sentence.

Whilst the Workshop still had plenty of work coming in, it was not enough to cover all their overheads. The democratic manner in which the Workshop accepted commissions from all comers, including low budget children's shows, made balancing the books unlikely. Ray White recalls that by spring 1992 the department's accounts were £72,000 in the red.[76] Drastic cuts had to be made.

Both Rays made enquiries about redundancy arrangements and on February 16th, Rupert Brun showed up with Fiona Sleigh, an engineer from the Maida Vale studios maintenance team, who was to work part-time as the new engineer at the Workshop. Ray White handed over his key, cleared his desk and then went home redundant. Ray Riley soon followed, the possibility of any further significant technical developments at the Workshop being brought to a sudden end.

That same year, Dick Mills, one of the Workshop's earliest remaining members, was also told his role would be ending in April but that if he left 'there and then' he would still get paid until that date, but Mills chose to stay on to complete his work, finally leaving on March 23rd, on the same day as Ray Riley.

Brian Hodgson left in 1995, in the hope that doing might save other jobs, but to no avail as Malcolm Clarke and Roger Limb also departed in the same year. In 1997 Peter Howell left after completing the theme for Michael Palin's *Full Circle*. Elizabeth Parker provided the incidental music, a project she had to complete as a freelancer after the closure of the Workshop.

Parker was the last composer to leave. Even now as she talks about it, the sorrow in her voice is evident.

"The engineer was there, I just shut the door and said 'Shall I give you the key then?' and he said 'That would be appropriate' and that was the last word that was said. I just walked out of the door and burst into tears. It was sad.

"They tried to say it didn't shut because John Hunt carried on doing restoration of sound but it then shut a year later with no hoo-hah. It was ridiculous. They had no idea how the thing would go full circle."[77]

Parker's words are bitingly true. In the same year that the Radiophonic Workshop closed its doors, Warp Records put out their first release from a Birmingham band called Broadcast, who were to extoll the virtues of the Radiophonic Workshop to a new generation around the world, whilst championing a more analogue approach to electronic music. The Workshop died just as a new generation was discovering its charms.

Mark Ayres came in to do the challenging job of cataloguing and preserving the Workshop's archive. Ayres' background included providing incidental music for *Doctor Who* during that series' final season (as a freelancer, not as a Workshop member) and he has also remastered a couple of older Radiophonic Workshop compilations for reissue on Silva Screen.

It was a quiet death, in the end, carried out behind the scenes and unannounced. To the extent that if the public were aware of the Workshop at all, their perceptions were so slanted towards the sixties and seventies that few even knew it was still going anymore.

We can only wonder at what the alternatives would have been. Perhaps if it had survived the Workshop could not only have kept up with the latest technology but also embraced its legacy and restored some older instruments to its arsenal of sounds. A new generation of composers who were directly inspired by the Workshop's history might have joined and reimagined it for a new century.

Of course, this is simply a dream of what might have been. The true legacy of the Radiophonic Workshop lives on in this generation of musicians and film-makers. It has spread far beyond the BBC and continues to challenge the notions of what a television programme should sound like.

Chapter Six – "A cross between a Meccano set and a chip shop"

Although the Radiophonic Workshop provided regular work and a steady wage, many chose to work outside it, both while employed by the BBC and afterwards. The commercially-focussed demands of the work led some to seek artistic satisfaction elsewhere, while others were simply interested in collaborating with musicians from outside the BBC – and, of course, there was also the possibility of a second income.

In fact, so successful have Radiophonic Workshop alumni proven, that it would be, at best, a half told history which did not spend some time examining their work away from the Corporation.

Least interestingly for those listeners looking for pure creativity and experimentation, library music did provide satisfactory (if limited) remuneration for the composer involved. For those not familiar with the concept, Library Music (also known as Production Music or Stock Music) was an easy way for TV and film producers to obtain music for their shows. Normally, composers retain 50% of the rights to their music and have a say over the manner in which the music can (or cannot) be used. The business model with Library Music, on the other hand, was that the composer and performers were paid a one off fee by a music library, and the library then retained all rights and ownership. The library would then earn all the royalties each time the music was broadcast.

In terms of more personal and wholly creative work, however, there is much to treasure in the combined back catalogues of former Workshop members.

It seems sensible to start our overview of these works with the activities of the first person to leave the Workshop; its founder, Daphne Oram. After resigning from the BBC in 1958, she immediately moved to form her own home studio in the imposing converted oast house, Tower Folly, in Kent. She primarily made her living through working on commercials and corporate films for clients such as Lego, Shell and Costain, but she also did a little film work, including providing the terrifying but subtle supernatural sounds for the classic 1961 chiller *The Innocents* as well as the marvellous music for the award winning 1963 short film *Snow* by Geoffrey Jones.

Perhaps her most famous and most well remembered post-Workshop piece is the advert she created for for Lego, *Lego Builds it*. Running for approximately thirty seconds, the piece begins with a typically American voice declaring 'It's Mission Moon for Studs Lego. He's off to pioneer the empty spaces of the moon with Lego, his wonderful building bricks.' Standard advertising fayre to this point, but as the American voice commands 'Build moon tractor' and the like, he's answered by a heavily reverbed young British boy, squeaking 'Lego builds it' over a background of unearthly sounds more commonly found in science fiction tv shows like *Space: 1999*. The effect is hugely memorable.

Oram also successfully obtained grants to develop her Oramics machine, a remarkable device that literally allowed her to 'draw' sound. Dick Mills remembers the feeling of ease and familiarity that Workshop people felt in Oram's studio, as the 'Heath Robinson' feel of the equipment matched that in Maida Vale (he also recalls someone describing the various objects on display as looking like a "*cross between a Meccano set and a chip shop*"[78]!). The Oramics machine had been a long term dream of Daphne's, having designed the machine in 1957 before the Workshop even existed. Even the demands of running the Workshop could not distract her from it, References in her personal correspondence from April 1958, describe the quest for financing for the machine, while she was still busy at the Workshop. Although no longer working, the machine has resided at the Science Museum in London since 2010.

Daphne Oram became something of an ambassador for electronic music in England, being interviewed on the topic and performing concerts with pieces such as "Four Aspects", performed at the Queen Elizabeth Hall in 1960. I wish there were contemporary accounts or reviews of this performance as while the piece begins gently enough with a muffled drum pattern and some high pitched distorted sounds, it grows and grows to a fearsome climax of intense and brooding dark noise that startles audiences even now when played on a concert P.A. system. With such frightening sounds, it is perhaps no surprise that the English recording industry took little interest in her work.

However, there was still a general curiosity about electronic music and Oram was interviewed occasionally for newspapers and television but generally treated like something of a novelty. Taking this curiosity to its natural conclusion, she did public demonstrations including some memorable moments where she would hand the microphone to audience volunteers and manipulate their voices.

Daphne wrote a book "An Individual Note Of Music" all about electronic music theory. The book is as singular as the music and the lady herself. On the one hand, it is a wealth of technical information and theory but at the same time is written in a light, witty style that could only be Daphne Oram. For all her intellect and innovation, she refuses to take herself or her topic too seriously, claiming at the start that the book is "for amusement" and including such light hearted comments as "even Winston Churchill was made of 50% water" which is not quite as odd as it seems out of context.

During her career, her only released music was her 1962 contribution to HMV's "Listen, Move & Dance" series. The "Listen, Move & Dance" series was – as the name suggests - music to which children could dance. This might sound odd until you consider the creative relationship modern dance has long held with the avant-garde. Leading New York choreographer Merce Cunningham regularly collaborated with his lover John Cage, pioneering what is known as "modern dance". With this in mind, it would make sense for children learning the skills of dance to know how to interpret modern, experimental music. Daphne herself composed music for the ballet "Xallaraparallax".

She embraced computer technology quite early on, from around 1977. She used both an Apple and an Acorn Archimedes computer. The work Daphne created on her computers is still being assessed – for instance, a prototype Oramics programme for the Archimedes was discovered among her discs, in addition to a wealth of music which the world has yet to hear.

Oram quit working for the BBC because she did not want to provide background music for drama, so while many of her peers contributed to music libraries, there is no record of Daphne ever having made such contributions and as she was under no contracts, she would not have needed to use a pseudonym.

If Oram's official releases were thin on the ground, to say the least, other former members of the Workshop were far more prolific. While still with the Workshop, Delia Derbyshire and Brian Hodgson had formed the organisation Unit Delta Plus with Peter Zinovieff. Zinovieff, the London born child of Russian aristocrats who fled the revolution, was co-owner of synthesizer makers Electronic Music Studios. He ran EMS with engineer David Cockerell and pioneering electronic composer Tristram Cary. Cary remains a legendary figure in English electronic music through his work on *Doctor Who* (he provided incidental music for most of the early Dalek stories) and Hammer films.

Unit Delta Plus was based in Zinovieff's townhouse in Putney. Formed in 1966 with the aim of creating and promoting electronic music, they organised an evening of electronic music in Newbury and took part in other events such as the 1967 *Million Volt Light And Sound Rave* at the London Roundhouse, where The Beatles' 'Carnival Of Light' had its only airing. However, Zinovieff was an inventor and composer, not a business man. The high costs of running Unit Delta Plus were not covered by their earnings and the unit was superseded by Kaleidophon.

In January 1968, Unit Delta Plus had given a lecture at Morley College in London. One attendee was American musician David Vorhaus who hit it off with Delia so dramatically that a week later they formed Kaleidophon Studio with Brian Hodgson. Kaleidophon ran for a year and a half, in which they created the "ESL104" album of sound effects for the Standard Music Library (with Delia Derbyshire and Brian Hodgson using the implausible fake names Li De La Russe and Nikki St. owing to their contract with the BBC). Ironically, it ended up being used by *Doctor Who* in the 1970s, not to mention a very large amount turning up on ITV's *The Tomorrow People*.

Kaleidophon also created soundtracks for Tony Richardson's production of *Hamlet* plus Greenwich Theatre's productions of *Medea* and *Macbeth*, as well as some work for commercials and the electronic sound for the magic mushroom scene in the film *Work Is A Four Letter Word*.

The most famous release to come out of Kaleidophon was *An Electric Storm*, the first album by David Vorhaus' electronic music project, White Noise. As both Hodgson and Derbyshire contributed to the album, they received sleeve credits which is one of the reasons why the record has remained popular and in print. Yet their contributions were quite minimal.

Sonic Boom said Delia told him that she only really contributed to 'Firebird' and 'Here Come The Fleas'[79] whilst Brian Hodgson stated that his only contributions were "*some bits and pieces for it and my voice is on it as the dead motorcyclist and the West Indian next door on "Here Come The Fleas". I did the stereo montage at the beginning and I found some of the lyrics from a writer I had worked with called John Renn-McDonald. It was basically David's project.*"[80].

An Electric Storm was released on Island Records in June 1969, around the same time that Kaleidophon wound up, and today is viewed as a classic and deeply influential album.

In 1972, Brian Hodgson left the Workshop. He cashed in his pension and founded Electrophon alongside composer John Lewis (who would go on to play on M's international hit 'Pop Muzik'). Here Brian recorded an album *In A Covent Garden* with long term *Doctor Who* composer Dudley Simpson, using Electrophon as an artists' name. The album came out on Polydor in 1973 and featured their synthesizer interpretations of classical music (or as Brian described it to me "pseudo-Wendy Carlos"[81].). A couple of tracks from the album even ended up being used on *Doctor Who*, in the 1977 Tom Baker story 'The Robots Of Death'.

1973 also saw Delia Derbyshire leave the Radiophonic Workshop, frustrated by the change to synthesizers and the quicker turnaround expected with them. Brian Hodgson wanted her to join Electrophon which she did briefly, working with him on the soundtrack to classic 1973 haunted house film *The Legend Of Hell House*. However, Hodgson recalled in an interview with magazine Wheel Me Out that "She was not in the right state; she was not really at her most creative at that point. She seemed almost on the edge of a breakdown, of really not knowing what she wanted to do and feeling the pressures were all too great"[82].

Unfortunately, the master tapes for their soundtrack are currently lost, though hopefully the resurgence in popularity of horror film soundtracks will lead to their re-discovery soon. Hodgson and Derbyshire were not merely providing a few sound effects but created the entire soundtrack – a soundtrack which has lost none of its power to unnerve and is one of the reasons why the film has endured so well over the decades.

Hodgson and John Lewis went on to release two albums under the name Wavemaker for Polydor, the 1975 album *Where Are We Captain?* and its 1976 follow up *New Atlantis*. They also created the horrendously rare 1975 album *Encore Electronic* for the Standard Music Library, which you would nowadays be hard pressed to find for less than £100.

Prior to joining the Workshop both John Baker and Brian Hodgson had also worked on Ridley Scott's debut short film *Boy and Bicycle* in 1958. Starring the director's own brother, Tony (later better known as a Hollywood movie director in his own right), Baker composed incidental music whilst Hodgson was billed as a "sound recordist". John Barry was so impressed with the twenty-five minute film that when asked for permission to use a piece of his music, he re-recorded it especially for Scott.

Baker worked under the pseudonym John Matthews for the Southern Library of Recorded Music and contributed some startlingly futuristic electronic music for them, the rhythmic qualities of which seem particularly prophetic. It was far more science fiction-esque than anything he did at the Workshop. He also worked on adverts and other commercial commissions. Fortunately, his work both inside and outside the Workshop has been given satisfyingly diligent releases in modern times.

Elizabeth Parker immediately began work on her own home studio after the Workshop closed, with help from Peter Howell. She created music for many more BBC TV documentaries, including another series with Michael Palin (*New Europe*) and worked for National Geographic, ITV, Channel Four, Sky and many more. She provided music for the DVD release of *Monty Python and the Holy*

Grail, not to mention many BBC Radio dramas and documentaries.

Richard Attree also set up his own studio and worked freelance. He created music for sit coms (Simon Nye's *Hardware* with Martin Freeman), documentaries (including *Gorillas Revisited* with Sigourney Weaver for BBC4) and even children's animations (cartoon series *Metal Heads*). He also began teaching composition for film and television at local colleges and via correspondence courses.

One last point. Whilst the modern record buying public has a very great interest in soundtracks, back in the sixties and seventies they lived very much in the shadow of popular music. There could well be far, far more work out there than that discussed above. Scores for forgotten movies, pseudonymous library work and forgotten adverts, each with something to add to the legacy of the Workshop.

Although here in the year 2015 a vast treasure trove of work *is* available, picked from the array of work done outside the Workshop, that catalogue is one that will continue to grow and grow over the years. All these decades later, any Radiophonic Workshop-related music collection remains only a work in progress.

Chapter Seven – "Ace performers with a Razor Blade"

Daphne Oram lived a fairly frugal, self-sufficient existence, her dietary requirements largely being met by the goats she kept. From 1982 to 1989 she taught weekly music classes at King's College in Canterbury, but she wasn't even seventy when a stroke forced her to retire and move into a nursing home. Her entire archive was taken in by Hugh Davis, the electronic composer and improviser who had worked with Stockhausen and all the great British improvisational composers. Davis was something of a hoarder, and the collection remained in his possession, undisturbed, until it was eventually joined by the archive of Lily Greenham (which itself included collaborations with Paddy Kingsland and a piece recorded in the Radiophonic Workshop with Richard Yeoman-Clarke).

Davis lived near Clive Graham of Paradigm Discs and the two made one another's acquaintance after a gig. They got on well, and Davis ended up recording a track for a compilation on Paradigm Discs. He also talked with Graham about doing something with the archives he held, but nothing concrete came of the idea beyond Davis bringing Oram's song "Four Aspects" over to Graham's studio to transfer it for the 2001 compilation *Not Necessarily English Music* (which saw Oram's classic track become a curious bedfellow of the fiercely improvisational likes of AMM, Derek Bailey, Cornelius Cardew and Evan Parker).

Daphne Oram passed away on January 23rd 2003, and Hugh Davis followed on January 1st 2005. Davis' widow wanted to get rid of all the things he had hoarded and so Clive Graham ended up temporarily taking in both Daphne Oram and Lily Greenham's archives. Turning these archives into the long discussed retrospectives he had talked about with Davis was an immense undertaking and it was not until 2007 that they eventually saw the light of day.

The double CD release *Oramics* finally saw a detailed profile of Oram's genius available to the listening public. The big secret was out. Over four years after her death, Daphne Oram was the toast of experimental music listeners the world over.

That same year, her archive moved to Goldsmiths University of London who, in partnership with the Sonic Arts Network, dedicated themselves to studying her archive and helping to understand the body of work she left behind. In 2008 she made a belated appearance on a Radiophonic Workshop compilation, *Retrospective*, which opened with one of her pre-Workshop tracks.

2011 saw two further Oram releases: *The Oram Tapes Volume One* another two CD compilation of even more material from her archive, and *Private Dreams and Public Nightmares*, a remix album by Andrea Parker and Daz Quayle created from the Oram Archive. 2013 saw Trunk Records reissue her *Electronic Sound Patterns* (from the *Look, Listen & Dance* series) on vinyl, and 2014 saw a further remix album, this time by Walls. There is still a lot to be heard in the Oram Archive, much more than has been released and though she has not been with us for more than ten years, her story, and her music, continues.

Delia Derbyshire worked as a radio operator for various companies after the Workshop, and had no further contact with the world of music until a chance encounter with Peter Kember, also known as Sonic Boom of the bands Spacemen 3, Spectrum and EAR. While working on his album *Forever Alien*, Boom decided to create a song in tribute, called simply "Delia Derbyshire". It was only when he noticed that the back of the pink album claimed that she was born in Coventry – co-incidentally where he was recording the album - that he decided to attempt to track her down.

"Now, Delia tells me there is no way this could have happened, and I'll beg to differ but she may well be right but I phoned up directory enquiries and asked for D Derbyshire in Coventry. They came back with one in Bedworth which is a little village outside Coventry. I rang up and asked for Delia Derbyshire but it wasn't her but the person said 'The lady you are looking for lives in Northampton'. Delia said there is no way that could have happened as she had no relatives and no-one knew where she was living. I'm not entirely sure that it isn't a figment of my imagination but I don't know how else I would have done it back then. This was before the internet was readily available and I couldn't have done a nationwide search for D Derbyshires, it would have taken forever.

"So, I asked directory enquiries for D Derbyshire in Northampton, got her number and I called her up. She was a little blown away to be getting some random call out of nowhere after decades of not doing anything. I said I was recording just down the road and I'd like to come over and meet you. She said 'I don't take visitors here but there's a little pub round the corner and I sometimes meet people there'. That's all she said at that point, though I later found out there was a good reason why she couldn't meet people at her house. Mostly that you couldn't get in there. I forget the area she lived in of Northampton but it was a weird little area. I went and met her and we got on. I kept in touch by phone."[83]

He would regularly play her what he was working on and get her feedback and guidance.

"One of my secret missions was to try and get her doing something again. She was reluctant because of all the changes in music and she had this horror of sampling. I would play her stuff that I was doing and she would give me feedback from 'Oh that was amazing' to 'Oh, that was outrageous! How can you do that to people?' She definitely got really turned on by music. She always kept up with experimental and modern classical.

"We used to talk for hours each night. She taught me pretty much everything I know about the principles of sound and synthesis. The way that sounds are made. She explained everything to me umpteen ways but if I didn't understand something, she would find another way to explain it. The

one collaborative piece I did with her was based on a type of synthesis where you take a bitmap and then the synthesizer takes that information as it scans across the photo and makes sounds. She loved it[84]."

However, Sonic Boom never quite convinced Derbyshire to take up music properly again. As Brian Hodgson recalls:

"When she got involved with him I was quite pleased as it sounded like someone who might get her to make music again. About two months later she rang me up saying 'This awful man, don't believe anything he says, he's stolen all my equipment, he's not to be trusted'. She not only rang me but also Mark Ayres and Clive, her partner. She was really quite vehement. She spoke to me about three months before she died

"The thing is that Delia could, towards the end of her life, get very enthusiastic about people and would then drop them or turn against them. She suddenly took up Daphne Oram. She found out she was in an old folks' home and went to visit her and was saying how dreadful it was how Oram had been treated. Three months later she was on the phone saying 'Oh she's just an evil old woman, full of bitterness' and would never speak to her again. She did the same with one of her very best friends. They did three plays together, went on holiday together and wrote each other very long intellectual letters and then she was on the phone to me saying 'Oh she is a bitter old woman, she hates me' and *[her friend]* did not know what had hit her. Even in the end, I was still trying to persuade them to restore contact.

"With Delia you'd get phone calls. They'd either be once a week or once every six months, occasionally once a year and when you picked the phone up, the conversation would actually carry on from where it had left off on the previous phone call! I adored her but she was difficult. At one point she did get very anti-me but it didn't actually get to the point where she refused to be in contact with me. I was not getting the phone calls and then I'd introduced her to someone who had written a thesis about her and Delia got onto the phone and gave me hell for introducing her to 'this stupid woman who had distorted everything I said'. So I spoke to her and she said she would send me the tapes of the interviews and I got them and on them there was Delia saying everything she had accused this woman of making up. She was erratic.

"I tried to get her involved with the electronic music society as it was then. They had done a project on computer music and were showing it off to people at York University. I managed to get Delia on that course, it was a weekend. They had all heard about her and hoping to meet her but apparently she just couldn't cope and spent most of the weekend in tears. I think she could have been bi-polar. There was certainly something of a manic depressive about her."[85]

Delia Derbyshire died on July 3rd 2001 from renal failure, following treatment for breast cancer.

Her music archive currently resides at the University of Manchester. There remains a considerable amount of organising, identifying and verifying to be completed (as recordings of friends' work seem to be mixed in among the unmarked tapes) but in 2014 a UK tour in her honour included a forty five minute sound collage drawn from her unreleased work held in the archive. While a single listen to that collage is insufficient to take everything in and provide a detailed description, there is no doubt that there is some wonderful Delia Derbyshire material waiting to be released.

After John Baker – the *'ace performer with the razor blade'*[86], in the words of Dick Mills - was sacked from the Workshop his alcoholism steadily worsened, and he never worked again, living entirely off his royalties. He was taken in by a neighbour, Daphne Walker, who although she owned three properties and appeared presentable, lived in extreme squalor. He contracted cirrhosis of the liver and put off seeking medical attention until it was too late. In 1996 he was diagnosed as having cancer of the liver and he died on February 7th 1997.

John Baker's music archive was taken in by his brother, the presenter Richard Anthony Baker. Richard sought the help of Alan Gubby from Nanny Tango who carefully transferred them all and tracked down much of John's unreleased work from the Workshop. Gubby then turned to Johnny Trunk who released two CD compilations in 2008 which helped cement John's reputation as a composer and arranger. A new compilation put together by Gubby, *The Vendetta Tapes* was released in 2015 on his label Buried Treasure.

Elizabeth Parker has for the time being, stopped making music. She explains:

"I worked very hard until around 2008 then I got to the end of my tether. Then we moved down to Cornwall. I would be out sailing with the family and I would get a phone call from an American producer asking me to change the middle-eight on something I had done for them. It was just intruding on my life and I decided to take a break for a moment and then that moment became a year which became three years. I am now making jewellery and inventing things but I haven't made music for five years.

"I will go back to it at some point. I had a brilliant computer with all the studio on it but it never quite felt right. It didn't feel honest. I think if I went back to it, I'd go back to pen and paper and real instruments. It served me very well for a long time, about thirty years, quite long enough. I love music, I love listening to music and hearing new composers. It's still there, I am just not doing it myself. The deadlines and people chomping at my heels all the time. The fees were going down and it just felt silly. There is an awful lot more to life than sitting in a studio writing music. I've embraced everything else and its wonderful, I'm really happy"[87]

Former Workshop members Dick Mills, Paddy Kingsland, Roger Limb and Peter Howell have begun performing live concerts as The Radiophonic Workshop. Joined by archivist Mark Ayres and a live drummer, they first performed in 2009 at the Roundhouse venue in London. After a hiatus, they resumed performing in 2013 and 2014, mainly playing music festivals around the UK. This line-up has reportedly been working together in the studio on an album with guests from the contemporary music scene, but at the time of writing no release date has been confirmed. Although not involved directly himself, having remained in retirement since leaving the Workshop, Brian Hodgson is very supportive of what they are doing *"I think it's terrific. I think what they're doing is fabulous. I went down to Peter Gabriel's studio in Bath to see them and they played me some of their stuff. It's brilliant."*[88]

2012 saw the launch of a new BBC Radiophonic Workshop, this time an online entity in collaboration with the UK Arts Council. Under the leadership of producer Matthew Herbert, the new entity seemed most active on its twitter account (@theradiophonic) although after a prolonged period of prolific tweeting, it has remained silent since May 2013. It seemed to be primarily concerned with sound itself as opposed to music. The last known project was taking sounds to a large mausoleum in Hamilton to benefit from the buildings extensive reverberation.

Whether or not these two new incarnations of the Workshop create anything of lasting note, there remains so much archival material that the world cannot possibly have heard the last of the Radiophonic Workshop.

Part Two: The Complete Reviews

1962

RAY CATHODE – TIME BEAT
Label: Parlophone
ID: 45-R 4901

Tracklist
A1 – Time Beat
B1 – Waltz in Orbit

Although not explicitly identified as being the BBC Radiophonic Workshop (the record label credits the songs composition to 'BBC Radiophonics'", even though Desmond Briscoe always hated the plural form of the word.), Ray Cathode, from as far back as April 1962, is widely regarded as being the first music release from the Workshop.

In fact, Ray Cathode is actually Beatles producer Sir George Martin (b.1926) and Maddalena Fagandini. 'Time Beat' itself is a little interval piece Maddalena had created and for this single Martin loops it and adds some jaunty, Greek-style arrangements over the top (the brief original is on the *21* and *Retrospective* albums). The B-side, 'Waltz In Orbit', is an original track started by Martin and finished off by Maddalena. There are some more of those Greek arrangements, but for the most part it sounds like a classic Jamaican dub track from 1974.

Both tracks are essential classics and if you are the sort of person who reads a book like this, then you need to own them in some form. The original 7" will set you back around £40 in good condition, but 'Time Beat' has been reissued as a B-side to the *Doctor Who* theme in recent years and, at the time of writing, you can buy both tracks in remastered form for twenty pence each from the Trunk Records website. Trunk have also included 'Waltz In Orbit' on their recent *Funny Old Shit Vol.1* compilation, alongside some original *musique concrète*, jazz and Bernard Cribbins - which works nicely.

DAPHNE ORAM – ELECTRONIC SOUND PATTERNS
Label: His Master's Voice
ID: 7EG 8762

Tracklist
A1 - Melodic Group Shapes 1
A2 - Melodic Group Shapes 2
A3 - Three Single Sounds Taken In Canon
A4 - Rhythmic Variation 1
A5 - Rhythmic Variation 2
B1 - Ascending And Descending Sequences Of Varying Nature

Label: Trunk Records (2013)
ID: TTT007

A side all Daphne Oram / B side all Tom Dissevelt

Tracklist
A1 - Melodic Group Shapes
A2 - Melodic Group Shapes
A3 - Melodic Group Shapes
A4 - Three Single Sounds Taken In Canon
A5 - Three Single Sounds Taken In Canon
A6 - Three Single Sounds Taken In Canon
A7 - Three Single Sounds Taken In Canon
A8 - Rhythmic Variations
A9 - Rhythmic Variations
A10 - Ascending and Descending Sequences of Varying Nature
A11 - Ascending and Descending Sequences of Varying Nature
A12 - Ascending and Descending Sequences of Varying Nature
A13 - Ascending and Descending Sequences of Varying Nature
A14 - Ascending and Descending Sequences of Varying Nature
A15 - Ascending and Descending Sequences of Varying Nature
A16 - Ascending and Descending Sequences of Varying Nature
A17 - Ascending and Descending Sequences of Varying Nature
A18 - Ascending and Descending Sequences of Varying Nature
B1 - Syncopation

B2 - Vibration
B3 - Whirling
B4 – Drifting

For forty years, Daphne Oram's only commercially available release was this 1962 seven-inch record. I say 'record' rather than 'single' advisedly, because on this little release are eighteen brief tracks created for Vera Gray's *Listen, Move & Dance* series (it can also be found on *Listen, Move & Dance* LPs), designed to give children something to dance to. Nothing here is longer than a minute and everything is nicely abstract to give the kids plenty of room to create their own interpretation.

Playful, shamelessly electronic and pretty in a funny little way.....imagine if Stockhausen had ever made a record your kids could enjoy. The melodies are simple but never corny and at one point Oram flits close to house music (on 'Rhythmic Variations Part 1'). In fact Part 2 is almost like a distorted hip hop beat.

Although the recent Trunk Records vinyl pressing (which saw it paired with a contemporary Dutch 7" release) is just about all sold out, it did see a widespread digital release, so you can grab this little gem as a legitimate download easily. It was also reissued at least twice in the sixties on *Listen, Move & Dance* compilations. Although only a short EP, the sheer range of the eighteen tracks creates a very fulfilling and pleasing listen. In contrast to the two epic Daphne Oram anthologies, this is a little gem you can easily fit into a busy life.

1963

GIANTS OF STEAM – RON GRAINER & THE RADIOPHONIC WORKSHOP
Label: Decca
ID: STO 8536

Tracklist
A1 - Rocket's First Run
A2 - Sunday Excursion
A3 - Working On the Line
B1 - The Victorians
B2 - Giants of Steam

Definitely more a Ron Grainer record than a Radiophonic one, this seven-inch crams in five pieces of music Grainer composed for a TV documentary about steam trains[89]. Underpinning Grainer's bouncy, dramatic music are beats created by Brian Hodgson, designed to sound like the rhythms of trains. It is, of course, amazing. Grainer, the hero of TV theme music, delivers big and bold but awesomely catchy big band sounds. This fantastic EP contains five tracks of Grainer at his peak, laying down the sort of insanely catchy brass music that made his reputation. The steam driven beats are so subtle as to sound almost like the work of a deeply intuitive drummer in places, or simply a well-chosen recording of a steam engine. It pre-empts Kraftwerk with the concept of using arranged percussion to imitate the sounds of transport[90].

Not an obvious Radiophonic work, but a hugely enjoyable slice of sixties' fun.

1964

BBC RADIOPHONIC WORKSHOP - DOCTOR WHO
Label: Decca
ID: F.11837 (NB reissued in 1972)

Tracklist
A1 – Doctor Who
A2 – This Can't be Love (by Brenda and Johnny)

As the BBC did not start its own record label until 1967, the *Doctor Who* theme made its vinyl debut on this seven-inch single from Decca. Presented in its original mono version, it sadly came with just a generic label sleeve.
The mysterious b-side is 'This Can't Be Love' by Brenda and Johnny, a jaunty sixties' pop song which seems completely out of place here. Nothing else was recorded by the duo, although the Johnny in question is said to be Johnny Goodison, also known as Johnny B Great, who wrote hits for Cliff Richard, Brotherhood of Man, The Bay City Rollers and others in the 1970s.

1966

DESMOND BRISCOE - ELECTRONIC SOUND PICTURES
Label: His Master's Voice
ID: CLP 3531 (As side 2 of Listen, Move and Dance No.4 LP)

Tracklist
(*Listen, Move and Dance No.4*)
B1 - A Wish / A Magic Journey
B2 - Machine
B3 - Discussion
B4 - Train
B5 - Smoke Rings
B6 - Mobile with Five Parts
B7 - Witches, Wizards, Alchemists, Sorcerers
B8 - Group Shapes
B9 - Journey into Space
B10 - Imaginary Creatures
B11 - Underwater Adventure
B12 - Dream

While Daphne Oram's own contribution to Vera Gray's *Listen, Move and Dance* series is widely known, this contribution to the same series from her old Radiophonic Workshop colleague, Desmond Briscoe, seems to languish in relative obscurity. A shame really, as it is deserving of a sympathetic listener. Created to stimulate the imagination of children while they work out their own little dance pieces, Briscoe plays to his audience by invoking trains, witches, magic journeys and underwater adventures. Of course, it was devised for the classroom, not the living room, and it would be foolish to claim it to be perfect for such altered circumstances.

It is equally clearly nowhere near as good as Oram's own entry in the series, but it is highly listenable and flows nicely. The sounds are mostly discordant and abstract with nothing much to write about in the mood or melody department, but never too noisy or overly aggressive. There are nice monster sounds for the listener's enjoyment, genuinely evoking a slimy beast roaring in a dungeon, and there are some fun alien sounds too. It is a pleasant little curio, although far from a classic album. In fact, you really need to be heavily into this kind of thing before you should bother with it. It's not bad, by any means, but neither is it anything special.

Briscoe's pieces are most easily found on the second side of *Listen, Move and Dance No.4* paired up with some fun percussion work from Vera Gray herself on the first side. Put together, they make a great album of curious old sounds. There is a series compilation that includes both Desmond and Daphne's contributions but it seems harder to find.

1968

BBC RADIOPHONIC MUSIC
Label: BBC Radio Enterprises
ID: REC 25M
Tracklist

A1 - Radio Sheffield (David Cain)
A2 - Radio Nottingham (John Baker)
A3 - Boys And Girls (John Baker)
A4 - Mattachin (Delia Derbyshire)
A5 - Pot Au Feu (Delia Derbyshire)
A6 - Time And Tune (John Baker)
A7 - Tomorrow's World (John Baker)
A8 - Reading Your Letters (John Baker)
A9 - Blue Veils And Golden Sands (Delia Derbyshire)
A10 - The Missing Jewel (John Baker)
A11 - Artbeat (David Cain)
A12 - Fresh Start (John Baker)
A13 - Christmas Commercial (John Baker)
A14 - Sea Sports (John Baker)
A15 - The Delian Mode (Delia Derbyshire)
B1 - The Frogs Wooing (John Baker)
B2 - Milky Way (John Baker)
B3 - Structures (John Baker)
B4 - New Worlds (John Baker)
B5 - Ziwzih Ziwzih OO-OO-OO (Delia Derbyshire)
B6 - Festival Time (John Baker)
B7 - The Chase (John Baker)

B8 - Towards Tomorrow (Delia Derbyshire)
B9 - Quiz Time (John Baker)
B10 - P.I.G.S. (John Baker)
B11 - Autumn And Winter (David Cain)
B12 - Door To Door (Delia Derbyshire)
B13 - Factors (John Baker)
B14 - War Of The Worlds (David Cain)
B15 - Crossbeat (David Cain)
B16 - Air (Delia Derbyshire)

This is an album more commonly known by its nickname, *The Pink Album* (on account of the pink-ish hues used on the cover). Originally compiled from existing work in 1968 as an album of library music for BBC departments to re-use as required, it was subsequently released to the public for the first time in 1970, and has remained a well-loved favourite ever since. It primarily features the work of John Baker, though with quite a few Delia Derbyshire classics and a tiny bit of David Cain.

Across this album you start to get quite a clear indication of John Baker's style. He makes clever, unusual arrangements, but based around a traditional compositional style. His catchy melodies find themselves being realised through an everyday sound such as blowing air over a bottle top and then pitch shifting the result into the different notes. His genius for such work hits a cynical peak with 'Christmas Commercial' where he uses the sound of a cash register chiming a sale to play the Christmas carol 'Oh Come All Ye Faithful'.

Delia Derbyshire contributes fewer tracks, but hits hard with what she does deliver. 'Blue Veils and Golden Sands' features the sound of a metal lamp being hit then manipulated into something soothing, otherworldly and hallucinatory, conjuring fantastical vistas. The unusually titled 'Ziwzih Ziwzih OO-OO-OO', on the other hand, is a warped electro track with weird hooks and beats, while 'The Delian Mode' is another classic piece of dark, abstract alienation, extracted from the *The Dreams* suite.

David Cain is oddly represented by some blood curdling sounds he created for a radio adaption of *The War of the Worlds*, a radio indent that sounds like John Baker, and two parts of his masterpiece *The Seasons,* segued together and robbed of vocals. It leaves the listener with less of sense of who Cain was, especially compared to Baker and Derbyshire, who succeed in stamping their own distinctive personalities onto the record.

This record is not just ground-breaking, though - it's also a huge pleasure to listen to. The sheer variety of moods and styles means it remains fresh throughout, dazzling the listener with something new every couple of minutes. It is difficult to argue with those who say that some of the greatest ever work realised at the Workshop is present here. It's simply an essential cornerstone of any Radiophonic collection.

The album has been remastered well for CD with a couple of bonus tracks. There is also a recent vinyl reissue from Music On Vinyl, which is easy enough to find. It's worth noting for vinyl lovers than in 2003 Aphex Twins' record label, Reflex, put out a four record set collecting both this and the 1975 compilation complete with the bonus tracks.

1969

NARROW BOATS - VOICES, SOUNDS AND SONGS OF THE CANALS
Label: BBC Radio Enterprises
ID: REC 56M

Tracklist
A1 – Untitled
B1 – Untitled

Although not usually counted as an official BBC Radiophonic Workshop release, this 1969 release was none the less the brainchild of Workshop boss Desmond Briscoe, and edited together at the Workshop by Dick Mills. Briscoe loved narrow boats and canals, so this release was very much a labour of love for him.

For the benefit of those not familiar, canals were man-made waterways and the main form of transporting cargo around the country before the development of the railways. Once a vital part of British industry and commerce, they are now preserved for pleasure trips, holidays and historical interest. Briscoe's passion was very timely. By 1969 commercial usage had died out but the BBC still had interviews in their archive with people who had worked on the canals, and the families who had travelled with them.

Briscoe and Mills create a sound collage from these interviews, from sounds of the canals and from the old songs that were part of the canal workers tradition, mostly sung by waterways' expert and canal historian, David Blagrove. There is a light touch of Workshop trickery as the sound of a narrow boat engine gets chopped and arranged into a rhythm to accompany some of Blagrove's canal ballads, but that is as noticeably Radiophonic as it gets.

Although in 1969 it might have been simply the sort of LP people would pick up for their Grandad's birthday, today it seems like a fascinating artifact for anyone interested in music and folklore. The songs and way of life that Briscoe sought to capture have vanished from the canals in my region, replaced by a strange mix of expensive holiday barges and people who cannot afford to get on the housing ladder buying them as cheap homes.

This album is as relaxing as it is culturally significant, and through its sheer normality contrives, paradoxically, to be the most unusual record you will find listed in this book.

An interesting footnote is that in 2014, David Blagrove was awarded an MBE in the Queen's birthday honours for services to Restoration of the UK Waterways, further proof of how shrewd Desmond Briscoe was in his choice of collaborator.

Incidentally, the 1969 BBC release is in mono. In 1975 a stereo version was released on Argo (a sub-label of Decca), created with the help of Richard Yeoman-Clark.

DAVID CAIN – THE SEASONS
Label: BBC Radio Enterprises
ID: RESR 7

Tracklist
A1 – January
A2 – February
A3 – March
A4 – April
A5 – May
A6 – June
A7 – July
A8 – August
B1 – September
B2 – October
B3 – November
B4 – December
B5 – Spring
B6 – Summer
B7 – Autumn
B8 – Winter
B9 - This Year

The BBC has long been involved in producing educational programmes and content especially for schools. This wonderfully bizarre record was put out in 1969 as just such an educational tool. David Cain created the music in the Radiophonic Workshop and poet Ronald Duncan wrote the words[91]. As the name suggests, this work is all about the changing of the seasons. A separate piece represents each month and then a further four for each season followed by a longer instrumental heralding the year.

This album was a very valuable and much sought after item in collector circles until Trunk Records gave it a much needed reissue on both vinyl and CD in 2012. Hats off to Trunk for this, as it really is a lost classic. Cain's music utilises catchy, nursery rhyme-style melodies arranged in stark, haunting electronics. This restrained minimalism is rendered all the more effective by those moments when he adds in some deep, churning low-end sounds to the mix. Even by Radiophonic Workshop standards, it is bewilderingly ahead of its time.

The simple, folkloric melodies compliment the nature imagery of the poetry, despite their high tech arrangements. In fact, it is hard not to think of the *Wicker Man* as this raw natural imagery, almost druidic in its devotion, gets hammered out for the kids. It certainly serves as one of the progenitors of the modern genre of 'hauntology', with its simple electronic melodies and mysterious aesthetics. However, as it was only released through the BBC Schools service, it fell off the Radiophonic Workshop discography for many years despite an instrumental amalgamating two of the tracks appearing on the original 1968 pink album.

Most album releases among the Radiophonic Workshop back catalogue are compilations of unrelated music, only a small handful are actual structured albums. 'The Seasons' is not just the best of that small group, it's also easily one of the best Radiophonic Workshop albums ever released. Halfway between The White Noise and *The Wicker Man*, this is an album that you really have to own.

WHITE NOISE – AN ELECTRIC STORM
Label: Island Records
ID: ILPS 9099

Tracklist
A1 - Love without Sound
A2 - My Game of Loving
A3 - Here Come the Fleas
A4 - Firebird
A5 - Your Hidden Dreams
B1 - The Visitation
B2 - The Black Mass: An Electric Storm in Hell

A simply perfect album of ground-breaking weirdo pop created at Kaleidophon. Although the project was definitely David Vorhaus' baby, its main selling point among record collectors was the presence of Brian Hodgson and Delia Derbyshire, credited with 'electronic sound realisation'.

Take one jazzy percussionist, three distinctive vocalists, and then utilise the studio to take the place of the band and orchestra. Whilst the album is a feast of wild, imaginative electronics the five songs on side one have a compositional style that harkens back to the hot, frothy jazzy style of the likes of Cole Porter rather than to contemporary rock n roll. Which might be why they are such disorientating fun!

It certainly makes it an impossible album to pinpoint to a date. The production is tomorrow, the songs are yesterday. Our tatty old vinyl copy still sounds simply out of this world on our surround sound hi-fi.

Over on side two, however, everything changes. 'The Visitation' is a lengthy slice of Procol Harem-style prog that keeps suddenly dissolving into nightmarish vortexes of sound. The lyrics are extremely un-nerving, with Brian Hodgson playing the role of a dead biker visiting his grieving lover following his accident.

Following this is the even darker 'Black Mass: Electric Storm In Hell' with its bizarre mix of occult chants, distorted jazz drumming, intense drones and screams. It's quite an unforeseen ending to an already unique album. As I said at the very start of the review, *An Electric Storm* is simply perfect.

Finally, a word of warning to those who dwell in family households: there is the sound of an orgy during the second song.

RUSSE/ST.GEORGE/VORHAUS – ESL 104 [aka The Tomorrow People]
Label: Standard Music Library
ID: ESL104

Tracklist
A1 - Lure of The Space Goddess
A2 - Battle Theme
A3 - Homeric Theme
A4 - Greek Concrete
A5 - Attack Of The Alien Minds
A6 - Gothic Submarine
A7 - Whirring Menace
A8 - Souls In Space
A9 - Time Capsule
A10 - London Lemons (Themes 1-9)
B1 - Restless Relays
B2 - Planetarium
B3 - Wet Asteroid
B4 - Way Out
B5 - Fresh Aire
B6 - Delia's Theme
B7 - Tentative Delia
B8 - Delia's Idea
B9 - Delia's Psychadelian Waltz
B10 - Delia's Resolve
B11 - Delia's Dream
B12 - Delia's Reverie
B13 - Delia's Fulfilment
B14 - Build Up To...
B15 - Snide Rhythms

An album known by two titles. Now best known as *The Tomorrow People*, its original title is simply *ESL 104* of the Standard Music Library.

An all-electronic album created by three individuals, sometimes in collaboration - leader of The White Noise, David Vorhaus alongside Nikki St George and Li De La Russe. A selection of short pieces of music, moods and sounds for use in film and TV. Library music was not publicly sold but instead supplied to film and tv production companies for a flat fee so they could use it on a royalty-free basis.

The reason for the second album title is that the cult tv show *The Tomorrow People* used the whole LP many times over for the show, leading to the reissue taking the show titled.

Should you have the financial means, you could hunt down a copy of the original 'ESL 104' which also includes 9 short versions of 'Oranges and Lemons' not included on Trunk Records widely released *The Tomorrow People* edition. Trunk also included the title music, composed by *Doctor Who* regular Dudley Simpson. So why are we featuring this release so prominently in our Radiophonic Workshop discography? Well, Nikki St George is actually Brian Hodgson and Li De La Russe is Delia Derbyshire. Oh, and also because this album is really very, very, very good. Nothing short of wonderful, in fact.

Made in 1969, presumably in their Kaleidophon studio, it does everything you would want an album of Delia & Brian's to do. It begins with Brian leaning towards extraordinary dark and moody space sounds and then drifts over to Delia creating surreal, twisted electronic waltzes and grooves. Finally, David comes in at the end for two horrifying and edgy blasts of electronic noise. It's a brief but very fulfilling album and an absolute must have for any Radiophonics head. At the time of writing, Trunk's CD version is still available and very cheap with a nice, vivid remaster. Trunk's vinyl edition, though, has been out of print for a while and sneaking up in price, although nothing crazy, and nowhere the cost of an *ESL 104* which will set you back over £50 for a dog-eared copy unless you get lucky.

JOHN PEEL PRESENTS TOP GEAR
Label: BBC Records
ID: REC52S

This wonderful compilation from 1969 was curated by the greatest English radio DJ of all time, John Peel, from radio sessions bands had recorded for his Radio 1 show (back then called *Top Gear*). It has two pieces of interest to Radiophonic collectors. Firstly, the opening of the album is over two minutes of Brian Hodgson and Delia Derbyshire weaving strange drones and manipulating John's voice. It is very brief and really just an amusing intro, but it is unmistakable as Derbyshire and Hodgson at work.

The second point of interest on here is 'Silence is Requested in the Ultimate Abyss', a track from Bradford collective The Welfare State which Peel says has been 'electronically treated' by The White Noise. It has even turned up on other compilations credited solely to The White Noise but the credits here clearly state that is was composed, written and performed by The Welfare State and produced by The White Noise under the direction of David Vorhaus. Derbyshire and Hodgson's involvement seems unlikely. It's a wild rock freakout with some electronic effects popping up suddenly at times and an edgy production sound. Definitely one for krautrock-lovers, although If its pure electronics you want this is not the place.

So what else is on here? There's the rather traditional (by Peel's later standards) rock of Sweet Marriage, a kind of Groundhogs-esque psychedelic hard blues rock band who contribute two tracks. The big treat on here though are four tracks from the well-loved British folk artist Bridget St John. These songs are not on any of Bridget's studio albums (apart from as bonus tracks on one CD reissue) and are all thoroughly lovely and essential. Eccentric sound artist (and Pink Floyd collaborator) R.Geesin contributes three wonderfully eclectic pieces blending old-time song, field recording, spoken word and Zappa-esque free vocal madness. If you like the first Faust album then you will be at home with his tracks

A strange piece of trivia about this album is that the sleeve was designed by Roy Curtis-Bramwell who would nearly 15 years later write the first book about the Radiophonic Workshop. This compilation has never been reissued and you would be extremely lucky to find a copy in good condition for less than twenty pounds. If you loved John Peel and the Radiophonic Workshop then you have to get this. If you don't really care for Peel or for 60s folk and experimental music then you would only get this if you've got the nutty completist bug.

PETER HOWELL AND JOHN FERDINANDO – ALICE THROUGH THE LOOKING GLASS
Label: Sound News Productions

Tracklist
A1 – The Alice Theme
A2 – March of the Chessmen
A3 - Jabberwocky
A4 – Dance of the Talking Flowers
A5 – Alice's Train Journey
A6 – Through the Looking Glass Wood
B1 – Dum and Dee
B2 – The Walrus and the Carpenter
B3 – Alice Meets the Night
B4 – A-Sitting on the Gate
B5 – Her Majesty Queen Alice
B6 – Whose Dream?

Label: Acme
ID: ACLN 1015CD

As SNP release, with the following bonus tracks:

March of the Chessmen Part 1
Alice Incidental Effects
Whose Dream? Section

Whose Dream? Section 2
Alice's Train
Alice's Train Part 2
Alice Incidental Effects Part 2
Jabberwocky (part)
A-Sitting on the Gate Section
Dance of the Talking Flowers (Instrumental)
Alice Incidental Music
Jabberwocky, Acoustic section
Whose Dream? (try-out)

This is the earliest released music from Peter Howell in his pre-workshop days and is a soundtrack for a theatrical production of the second Alice story. His early output is often labelled 'psychedelic folk', which is a fair approximation of the style of music but perhaps slightly misleads about the construction of the music. This is actually music composed by Peter Howell and performed by him and John Ferdinando on a wide variety of instruments, mostly traditional but there does appear to be some electric organ interjecting occasionally on tracks such as 'The Walrus and the Carpenter'.

    The mood for this production is firmly rooted in Alice's strange world, a pastoral paradise, an Elysium field of fun and frolics. The compositions are joyful and the arrangements immensely folky. There's a lovely live sound to the piano, which sounds as though the microphone were alone in an old empty house with only the player for company. The flute and autoharp conjure up childhood wonders.

'Jabberwocky' is sung with acoustic guitar and sudden wonderful bursts of extra arrangements explode into life towards the end. I am a huge fan of Lewis Carroll's work and this poem is one of my favourites, something I am very protective of, and the idea of someone turning it into a folk song horrifies me on paper, but Howell and Ferdinando actually do the impossible and take this great piece of art and translate it faithfully and honourably into a very different medium.

The album also includes snatches of dialogue from the production which sounds like it was quite a fun, witty performance and nicely enhances the origins of the music. If you are a fan of the eccentric and complex psychedelic folk sounds of the Incredible String Band or Witthüser & Westrupp then this will definitely suck you in. Another good reference point would be Trunk Records wonderful compilation album *Fuzzy Felt Folk* with its intricate whimsy. Maybe even a cleaner cut Kevin Ayers.

I am very glad to say this album has been reissued a few times including a fairly recent CD version, so you should have no problems purchasing a reasonably priced copy and I heartily suggest that you do.

PETER HOWELL & JOHN FERDINANDO - TOMORROW COMES SOMEDAY

Label: Sound News Productions
ID: SNP97

Tracklist
A1 - Title Theme
A2 - Someone Like You
A3 - March of the Civil Servants
A4 - Bluebottle Stripe
A5 - Setting Sun
A6 - On Location
B1 - Everything has its Place
B2 - Fishing
B3 - Tomorrow Come Someday
B4 - Love Theme
B5 - Honesty
B6 - Windfall Wood

Sleevenotes

"A musical comedy shot on location in the Sussex village of Lurgeshall, during August 1969 and featuring Emma Stacey, Michael Pipe, Andrew Lowcock, Andrew Crofts, Leslie Starkey and David Horlock'

Another 1969 soundtrack from Howell/Ferdinando but this time for a film and you can tell right away what a perfect fit for Radiophonic Workshop Peter Howell turned out to be. His understanding of the visual medium and what the composer can add to it is so clear on here. Obviously the country setting and a main character being a folk singer makes for fertile ground for his early work but the film also gives him chances to create ironic marches and satirical songs.

Wisely steering clear of popular music conventions of the day, the soundtrack has a pleasingly timeless feel to it, delving into musical styles still fertile and vibrant in the present day. Yes, if you were looking to shove it in into a pigeonhole then you could use the old 'psychedelic folk' tag but really this is just excellent soundtrack work. It's a whimsical, feel-good film and the soundtrack captures that perfectly, glowing with English summer charm and the spirit of youthful defiance and innovation.

The excellent Acme label has done much to make these early Howell/Ferdinando works widely available and nowhere is their work more sumptuous than for this soundtrack as they have not just given us a vinyl repress and a CD remaster, but the CD version comes with the original film on DVD too! To give new life to a lost, obscure British film is an honourable undertaking, comparable to what the BFI have been doing with their Flipside range and I can only give this the highest recommendation possible for every possible reason.

1970

AGINCOURT – FLY AWAY
Label: Merlin Records
ID: HF10

Tracklist
A1 – When I Awoke
A2 – Though I May be Dreaming
A3 – Get Together
A4 – Joy in the Finding
A5 – Going Home
A6 – All my Life
A7 - Mirabella
B1 – Take me There
B2 – Lisa
B3 – Dawn
B4 – Barn Owl Blues
B5 – Kind Sir
B6 – Through the Eyes of a Lifetime (Parts I-III)

Agincourt was the first released project from John Ferdinando and Peter Howell that was not a soundtrack. Dispensing with simple background music, they fully embrace the medium of song with classic boy and girl vocals in harmony, writing roughly half the songs each. Joining them is the singer Lee Menalau with her strong, beautiful voice. At first it sounds like the classic West Coast psychedelic pop sound and then some clever little arrangements sneak in that distinguish it from other followers.

Clocking in at forty minutes - about the most you can reasonably fit on a single LP – it's clear the duo were at their peak at this time. If you have never dug deep into this kind of music before and only know the big studio productions of The Beatles and the Beach Boys then you need to know this was made with a far smaller budget and it does show a little bit. Yet for all the small label limitations, the writing, playing and arranging is all first rate and shines despite a little studio murk.

The term 'psychedelic folk' gets thrown at these Howell/Ferdinando recordings a lot ('a gently magnificent slice of cosmic folk-rock', according to one recent review[92]) but it's a label which really does not suit them. While the arrangements are colourful it's not a hazy drug record; rather it's a record full of life and energy. As for folk, that's even wider of the mark, - it really is very much a well-played pop record with a little folk in its DNA.

Admittedly, there's some acoustic guitar and even a bit of flute, but the drumming is quite jazzy and the whole thing feels like a songwriter's album, complete with some great arrangements.

A couple of the intros display a little electronic trickery and sounds but it really is only a little splash of sound, for the most part this is a really nice, toe-tapping, catchy pop album with sophisticated arrangements. It has been reissued a few times on CD and vinyl, although the first CD reissue was in 1994 when digital remastering was far behind modern standards, and collectors are advised to seek out the 2002 ACME re-issue, which adds a couple of bonus tracks (a different take of 'Going Home' and a stereo mix of 'Though I May be Dreaming').

1971

TRANE – WAGGONER'S WALK
Label: BBC Records
ID: RESL5

Tracklist
A1 - Waggoners' Walk
A2 - Jenny's Song
B1 - Ragged Bird
B2 - Mansion Of Cards

This funny little 7" EP is music from an old BBC Radio 2 soap opera that ran from 1969 to 1980. There have been a few bands called Trane but this one was led by songwriters Brian Wade and Anthony Cliff. Wade and Cliff would go on to write songs for *very* middle of the road acts like Elaine Paige, Samantha Jones and Giggles so it's no huge shock that there's a very mainstream soft rock pop sound to the first side (in fact, that element has turned into a bit of a guilty pleasure for me!). The music on this EP was produced by Brian Hodgson and Paddy Kingsland while Hodgson was on attachment to BBC Records. Apparently, they managed to persuade the show's producer to write a pop group into a storyline so they could make this record.

The reason everyone wants to own this four track EP, however, is the last track, 'Mansion Of Cards', with its swooping synth noises and dancefloor drums. It's an absolute gem that has found its way onto many compilations and into many discerning DJs setlists. Unfortunately, the record is a little bit on the rare side (having been distributed alongside kettles and ovens to hardware stores rather than through conventional record shops) but well worth seeking out. There are some unsourced reports online that Delia Derbyshire was involved but when I asked Brian Hodgson he said this was wrong[93].

DAVID MUNROW AND THE EARLY MUSIC CONSORT OF LONDON – PLAY MUSIC BY DAVID CAIN FROM FOUR RADIO PLAYS
Label: BBC Records
ID: REC91S

Tracklist
A1 - The Hobbit
A2 - Hajji Baba
B1 - The Jew of Malta
B2 - Much Ado about Nothing

Well, you probably see the title of this one and ask the question 'but is this radiophonic?' Unfortunately, the answer is 'it's not clear!' David Cain was certainly a member of the Radiophonic Workshop when he composed his scores for *The Hobbit*, *Hajji Baba*, *The Jew of Malta* and *Much Ado About Nothing*. The sleeve notes state 'More often than not the purely orchestral music has been treated electronically in the BBC Radiophonic Workshop before being finally added to the production' but the credits do not make it clear if the music contained on this release are presented before or after such treatment. The only clues are the credits - 'Original music by David Cain, BBC Radiophonic Workshop. Record Produced by David Cain' which suggests it might be after electronic treatment.

There is also an advert for the 'pink album' on the back, which at least hints at a perceived shared audience.

Personally, I find the tracks contained here sounds like my idea of perfect medieval music. Though I must confess myself unfamiliar with the true sound of a 'Tranverse Flute' or 'Bass Racket' or even a 'Chinese Shawms' (which my spellchecker seems to be unfamiliar with too). It all sounds to me like a skilled ensemble of nine musicians playing original music in a medieval style.

So, electronic intervention or not, this is definitely not electronic music. What it is, though, is very good. By cherry-picking from the soundtracks of four different plays, it actually packs in an enormous amount of variety. Sad laments, happy celebrations, declarations of love and hate, themes for war and peace – they are all here. Not surprising when you consider these are the themes for a children's fantasy story, an Arabian legend, a tale of racism and murder and Shakespeare's finest romantic comedy!

This may not strictly be electronics, but this is early music and is definitely not a bad record and would sit nicely between *The Seasons* and The Third Ear Band in your record collection

1972

HARPER/RUSSE/ST GEORGE – ELECTROSONIC
Label: KPM Music
ID: KPM 1104

A 1972 library music album credited to Don Harper (an Australian composer, best remembered for the music from the 1969 *Doctor Who* story 'The Invasion'), Russe (Delia Derbyshire) and St George (Brian Hodgson). [94]

Brian Hodgson has stated the project was very much led by Harper, whom he took a dislike to and suspected of just using Delia so he could work on electronic music. The album seems to consist of a couple of pieces by Hodgson and quite a few by Derbyshire, all being used as backing tracks for Harper to arse around horrendously over. As a lover of experimental music, I do not find discordant music offensive, but this sounds like someone playing around with a synthesizer with no idea of what they are doing or how it works.

A couple of tracks are very subtle, minimal and delicate, so are probably just the work of Derbyshire or maybe Hodgson without Harper messing around with random synth shoving. Obviously, Harper was a fantastic composer when it came to jazz and big band sounds but here he is way out of his depth and floundering badly.

Although there are a few moments of greatness and some further moments of acceptability, this is far and away the worst record Delia has been involved with. Her unreleased archive contains far more striking work than this album...but it has got Delia Derbyshire and Brian Hodgson on it so really, you have to own it.

The vinyl edition was reissued three times on different coloured vinyl so it usually goes for a reasonable price but the CD version with its fairly functional remastering seems to go for almost as much as the original 1972 library issue! Don't do it!

SOUNDS FROM..... EMS – SYNTHI
Label: Electronic Music Studios
ID: N/A

Tracklist
A1 – The Axons Approach (Dudley Simpson)
A2 - Untitled Canon (David Vorhaus)
A3 – Plays Haydn (Peter Zinovieff)
A4 – Dance From "Noah" (Delia Derbyshire)
A5 – BBC Radio Solent (Delia Derbyshire)
A6 – BBC Radio Teeside (Malcolm Clarke)
A7 - An Ornithologist Who Is Trying To Study Birds But Is Interrupted By A Wasp, A Lawnmower And A Lady Trying To Sing (Unknown Artist)
B1 – The War Of The Worlds (Extract) (Malcolm Clarke)

B2 - Seascape (Brian Hodgson)
B3 - Continuum (Extract) (Tristram Cary)
B4 - January Tensions (Extract) (Peter Zinovieff)
B5 - Thing For Two VCS3s (Extract) (David Vorhaus)
B6 - Dover Castle (Dudley Simpson)

This little flexi disc starts off with a snatch of Brian Hodgson's intimidatingly bold realisation of 'The Axons Approach' by Dudley Simpson to demonstrate the power of the EMS Sythi 100. From there, we are swiftly onto the EMS synth sales pitch which intercuts each track. Following that is David Vorhaus with an elegant, spacey piece of sci-fi classical music, then Peter Zinovieff plays a slice of reimagined Haydn getting further and further from the score with wilder and wilder arrangements. You would be forgiven for thinking this is the peak, bu then comes the absolute killing blow of Delia Derbyshire's 'Dance from Noah', a euphoric piece of acid house far before its time. We get her very brief BBC Radio Solent news intro, a swift blast of utopian electronic fanfares, before Malcolm Clarke's little piece for Radio Teeside manages to make synths sound like Mozart and ship's foghorns at the same time. The final piece on side A is a sound effects demonstration of 'An Ornithologist Who Is Trying To Study Birds But Is Interrupted By A Wasp, A Lawnmower And A Lady Trying To Sing' which actually just sounds like a rowdier version of Cluster's synth wig-outs (no artist named, sadly).

    Side two kicks off with more of David Cain's disturbing *War of the Worlds* sound effects, presumably of a Martian army destroying a city. It really does sound like the electronic end of the world. Brian Hodgson's 'Seascape' resembles some gentler passage of an abstract noise improvisation from forty years later, before an extract of Tristram Cary's 'Continuum' kicks off like a more incendiary high-end moment of an abstract noise improvisation also from forty years in the future. Peter Zinovieff provides a contrasting low end moment of deep, tense rumblings, David Vorhaus presents a piece for two VCS3s which is quite a groovy little bit of space funk, the disc culminating with 'Dover Castle', Brian Hodgson's sparkling arrangement of Dudley Simpson's piece for 'The Mind Of Evil'.

Any musician who listens to this twelve minute flexi-disc will be hard pushed to avoid going hunting for an EMS synth or at least an app version. Those less musically gifted will merely find themselves glowing in appreciation of a group of individuals so far ahead of their time. Be warned - it's a bit of a pain to find, I'm afraid.

1973

BBC RADIOPHONIC WORKSHOP - DOCTOR WHO (STEREO VERSION)
Label: BBC Records
ID: RESL11

Tracklist

A1 - Dr Who (Stereo Version of the BBC TV Theme Music)
A2 – Reg

This 1973 single is the collectors' choice when it comes to owning the *Doctor Who* theme. First, the theme has been given the stereo treatment. Secondly, it comes in a wonderful picture sleeve showing the TARDIS in front of some kind of etch-a-sketch pattern. And third, the font used for *Doctor Who* is rather memorable.

The B-Side is Paddy Kingsland's cheery 'Reg', a very catchy, heavily synth driven number that featured on the *Fourth Dimension* album that same year. It doesn't really match up very well with the A-side's dark mood and music concrete techniques but is more apt than the random pop song Decca shoved onto the b-side of their version.

BBC RADIOPHONIC WORKSHOP - FOURTH DIMENSION
Label: BBC Records
ID: RED93S

Tracklist
A1 - Scene & Heard (Radio 1)
A2 - Just Love (BBC TV)
A3 - Vespucci
A4 - Reg (BBC African Service)
A5 - Tamariu (BBC TV)
A6 - One-Eighty-One (Radio 4)
B1 - Fourth Dimension (Radio 4)
B2 - Colour Radio (BBC Radio Leeds)
B3 - Take Another Look (Radio 4)
B4 - Kaleidoscope (Radio 4)
B5 - The Space Between (Radio 3)
B6 – Flashback

Originally conceived as a split album between Paddy Kingsland and John Baker, this ended up having to be all the latter's work due to Baker's declining health. Of the twelve tracks included, two are original to the album and the other ten are themes and indents created for BBC TV and radio, given stereo sound and extended into song length. There have been some confused reporting of Kingsland as bringing 'pop' music to the Workshop but it is quite obvious on here that jazz and soul were more of an influence, especially when you hear some drumming on here such as on 'Vespucci'. The 'pop' term is presumably because there is a lot of guitar on here. Nearly every track has some form of rhythm guitar, usually in the background beneath the synths but only on 'Scene & Heard' (which was created for Radio 1) can you hear a little bit of modern rock sneaking it over a majorly danceable beat.

Mostly, though, it seems more like the Morricone-tinged world where jazz and classical music collide, filtered through Workshop technology. A track Kingsland made for EMI in 1974 even ended up on a compilation from distinguished jazz label Blue Note[95].

Side one is easily the funkiest of the entire Radiophonic Workshop output, with songs that could fit into most DJs sets at some point and some classic grooves. Original song 'Vespucci' usually features in the Radiophonic Workshop's live sets with its guitar and drum rhythms especially suited to the live line-up. Side two is more traditional synthesizers, including a haunting theme for 'Kaleidoscope' and the easy listening of 'The Space Between'. *Fourth Dimension* offers something you will not find anywhere else in the Workshop's discography.

It is yet to be released on CD apart from a recent promo, which is ironic as the front cover looks like an exploding CD. It is to be hoped, given the promotional release, that an official CD is imminent, however.

2014 saw the album given the deluxe 180g vinyl treatment whilst older copies should not set you back too many pennies for a very playable copy. *Fourth Dimension* is another one of the essential cornerstones of any Workshop collection.

MOONBASE 3 / THE WORLDS OF DOCTOR WHO
Label: BBC Records
ID: RESL13

Tracklist
A1 - Moonbase 3 (Theme Music of the BBC TV Series)
B1 - The Worlds of Dr Who (Incidental Music from the BBC TV Series)

The theme tune for tense, gloomy 70s sci-fi series *Moonbase 3* is credited as composed by Dudley Simpson and realised by Dick Mills, but the influence of dear old Ron Grainger can be felt just as strongly as either (I mean that as a compliment, incidentally). Ominous big bass drums are accompanied by some very dramatic brass and underpinned by what sounds very like a moog. It's no wonder the series was perceived as pessimistic, really, because even the theme tune come across like a harbinger of disaster and devastation (plus little spacey bits of moog and some eerie electronic drones at the end).

Meanwhile, over on the b-side 'The Worlds Of Dr Who' is an insane, extended big band stereo version of the main music from the *Doctor Who* serial 'The Mind Of Evil', as heard in its original form on the *21* LP. It begins with a strange, dark wave of tropical electronics before building up into the familiar electronic arrangement that Simpson realised at the Workshop with Dick Mill's help. Then, in a sudden surprise, horns move to centre stage and the tune dissolves in an electronic whirl. It's a very audacious bit of work and marks this one out as another essential purchase.

IAN CARR & NUCLEUS - LABYRINTH
Label: Vertigo
ID: 6360 091

Tracklist
A1 - Origins
A2 - Bull Dance
A3 - Ariadne
A4 - Arena
B1 - Arena (Continued From Side One)
B2 - Exultation
B3 – Naxos

Ian Carr was a Scottish jazz musician and band leader who had been releasing music since 1961. Nucleus was his jazz-fusion meets prog rock band, founded in 1970, and travelling similar lanes to Canterbury's Soft Machine and even Miles Davis, who was in his *Bitches Brew* phase at the time.

The latter comparison is, in fact, the stronger one, as Nucleus took a deeply jazzy approach to prog. The British jazz scene has long been overlooked, burdened by the albatross of Acker Bilk's huge hit 'Stranger on the Shore' but Nucleus shatter the myth of British jazz as coming from a pedestrian and conservative tradition.

Labyrinth was the first Nucleus album to be released after Carr had lost some key players to The Soft Machine. Deciding not to bother replacing the guitarist, he went ahead and made *Labyrinth* as a straight up jazz fusion album, with the only hint of prog coming from the suggestion that this is a concept album, albeit one in which the theme isn't entirely clear.

No strangers to an EMS VCS3, for this album Carr convinced Paddy Kingsland to play it for them, but personally I have only been able to detect Kingsland on 'Arena', a track split between the end of side 1 and the start of side 2. It's a wonderful Sun Ra-esque piece of spiritual space jazz that starts off minimalist and plinky-plonky on part one and then explodes into a supernova jazz breakdown during part two, before going off into Heliocentric nothingness towards the end.

Unfortunately, that seems to be it for Kingsland and the Radiophonic connection but there is so much more to this explosion of colourful, wild jazz than a simple, obsessive need to tick off Workshop connections. Norma Winston's wordless vocals are extraordinary, the tunes are always inventive and the players are all first rate. If you like your jazz adventurous and nimble then this is a must for you.

Just don't expect any minotaurs (or David Bowie in a bad wig and posing pouch!).

ELECTROPHON (aka THE UNEXPLODED MYTH) – IN A COVENT GARDEN (aka FURTHER THOUGHTS ON THE CLASSICS)

Label: Polydor
ID: 2823 210

Tracklist
A1 - Arrival of the Queen of Sheba
A2 - The Girl with the Flaxen Hair
A3 - The Flight of the Bumble Bee
A4 - None but the Weary Heart
A5 - Allegro
A6 - Greensleeves
A7 - Sabre Dance
B1 - Skaters Waltz
B2 - Serenade
B3 - Moto Perpetuo
B4 - Anitra's Dance
B5 - Hall of the Mountain King

When I spoke to Brian Hodgson for this book, he described this album as 'pseudo Wendy Carlos' and it is true that the spectre of Carlos' 1968 album *Switched On Bach* does haunt this release. Her album of moog interpretations of Bach divided the critics but was a huge commercial success, meaning that by the time this record came out, the world had already heard 'The Moog Strikes Bach', 'Chopin A La Moog', 'Switched On Gershwin', 'The Unusual Classical Synthesizer' and 'Everything You Always Wanted to Hear on the Moog* (*But were afraid to ask for)' among others. In such a crowded marketplace, this similar work from Brian Hodgson and regular *Doctor Who* composer Dudley Simpson slipped by almost unheralded. A couple of tracks made it into the *Doctor Who* serial 'The Robots of Death' but that was about the extent of the album's contemporary fame.

Which is a shame, because Simpson and Hodgson are no dilettantes and they clearly have every skill needed to deliver on a project like this. There is nothing crass or lacking about their work on this album, with some very imaginative arrangements on offer here - the more upbeat numbers, for instance, positively bubble with energy as Simpson and Hodgson's new versions give them room to breathe rather than stifle them in the transition. Conversely, they display amazing delicacy with their take on 'The Girl with The Flaxen Hair', coaxing some lovely sounds out of their studio, and soothing the listener - only to follow up with an outrageously mad version of 'The Flight of The Bumblebee' whose titular hero seems transmogrified into some strange metallic wasp.

For me, though, the highlights are the sublime 'Greensleeves' with its gentle electronic sounds and, at the opposite end of the spectrum, the absolutely outrageous blast through 'Hall of the Mountain King', a track that makes me grin from ear to ear every time with its deep bassy sounds. This is yet another LP that you should own.

There has been no CD version yet but the vinyl has come out a few times (as you can tell by the variations in both artist name and album title) so shouldn't trouble your wallet too much for a respectable copy.

BOBBY LAMB AND THE KEYMEN – Self titled
Label: BBC Records
ID: ROUNDABOUT 101S

Tracklist
A1 - Alone Again, Naturally
A2 - Fool on The Hill
A3 - The Summer Knows
A4 - Kiskadee
A5 - Siobahn
A6 - Cinnamon and Cloves
B1 - Harlem Nocturne
B2 - Aquarius
B3 - Wave
B4 - Watch What Happens
B5 - Myreed
B6 - Day By Day

This LP is about as easy listening as it gets. Trombone player Bobby Lamb has his ten-piece band (which includes harp player Dave Snell) and for the most part plays it quite mellow. His take on 'The Summer Knows', for instance, resembles a track from a 1970's European soft porn film and it's not exactly an outlier.

But, of course, the band is packed with very fine musicians and to dismiss this album as pure cheese would be to completely miss the point. As is the tradition in this genre, you get some imaginatively arranged cover versions of well-known standards and a couple of original compositions such as the exotica of 'Kiskadee'.

That said, their Hammond heavy take on the Beatles 'Fool On The Hill' will sweep you off your feet with its sudden explosions into amphetamine rhythms but for the most part this is slow grooves for Bobby's trombone to gently purr over.

So, what is the Radiophonic Workshop connection? Once again, it's Paddy Kingsland, who is credited with arrangements and radiophonic treatments on Lamb's version of 'Aquarius'. Kingsland creates a stark, twinkling sci-fi intro which promptly halts the moment the band begin a particularly lame, elevator music arrangement of the song (from the musical *Hair*). Kingsland's trippy little effects make a welcome return later in the song, but sadly find themselves buried under the worst track on the album. We get a reprise of the intro at the end for a few seconds and then it's back to business as usual.

In summary, while this is not a bad album at all and of great interest to easy listening enthusiasts, its Radiophonic appeal is particularly limited. If you have no interest in trombones, gentle cha-cha-cha rhythms or lounge music then you would be advised to keep well away from this. If you love all of that, of course, then go for it.

ITHACA – A GAME FOR ALL WHO KNOW
Label: *Self released*
ID: N/A

Tracklist

A1 - Journey (Destruction - Rebirth - Patterns Of Life)
A2 - Questions (Did You Know - Will We Be Alive)
A3 - Times (Seven Seasons - The Path - Given Time)
B1 - Feelings (Look Around - I Want To Feel You)
B2 - Dream (Story Of Our Time - Beneath This Sky)
B3 – Journey II (A Game For All Who Know)

Bonus tracks on CD reissue (ACME, ACLN1003CD, 2004)

All My Life (Stereo)
The Poem (Stereo)
Peace of Mind (Stereo)

Ithaca is essentially, an expanded Agincourt. The core Agincourt trio of Peter Howell, John Ferdinando and singer Lee Menelau (now known as Lee Menelaus although perhaps the previous spelling was a typo, as one of the Agincourt reissues changes the spelling to Menelaus) remain but drummer Brian Hussey has now been officially added to the line-up, alongside a fifth member named Brian Garrett on 12-string guitar.

This release certainly has more of an ensemble feel than the Agincourt album, with the songs seeming more like pieces developed by a band instead of having simply been arranged and composed in isolation. The song writing is better too, with many songs instantly lodging in your head.

There is no fancy sonic trickery on display until the final track, when we get some dazzling guitar work slowly faded in over a swirling abstract bit of sonics. The guitar takes over, the sonics halt, and just as the guitar is about to go all out flamenco it gets overtaken by a sample of a NASA space craft launching and a slurry of weird synth sounds.

Interestingly, the album was self-released in a limited edition private pressing, and while Howell and Ferdinando worked together on one more album as 'Friends', that was not to see the light of day for thirty years as Howell joined the Radiophonic Workshop. The opening of that new door appears to have closed the door on the era of Howell and Ferdinando, which is a pity but perhaps unsurprising (not least because a band with three different names over only four albums is not likely to build up a dedicated following too easily!)

A Game for all Who Know has been reissued a few times on both CD and LP so should be easy enough to track down.

1974

JOHN BAKER – DIAL M FOR MURDER
Label: BBC Records
ID: RESL20

Tracklist
A1 – Ricochet (Norrie Paramor and The Midland Radio Orchestra)
B1 - Theme Music from BBC TV's *Dial M for Murder* (John Baker)

Hidden away on the b-side of something unrelated is this startlingly techno-ish theme tune. Hints of jazz and spy soundtracks meet with some great electronic beats. It features on the first John Baker anthology on Trunk Records but it is nice to have it on a vintage seven inch.

ELECTROPHON - ZYGOAT
Label: Polydor
ID: 2383 270

Tracklist
A1 - Leaves Of Sand
A2 - Zygoat
A3 - Ybur Knom
A4 - Pillar of Salt
A5 - Movement to the Earth

A6 - Seeds Cast to the Wind
B1 - Zy-Clone
B2 - Ybur Doon
B3 - Zygomania
B4 - The Ladder of Zeugma
B5 - The Libran Sea
B6 - Perseverance Furthers

The second album credited (albeit only discreetly on the spine) to Electrophon, *Zygoat* sees them working solely on music composed by Burt Alcantara. To be strictly accurate, the music in question was written by Alcantara for a ballet and then reworked into record format by the Electrophon studio. The composer had been working with a New York modern dance company, The Works, since 1971, composing mostly for synthesizer, so knew his work was in safe hands at Electrophon.

  The results are quite surprising. Almost from the start on it hits the kind of intricate keyboard acrobatics and complex arrangements you'd normally associate with the likes of Rick Wakeman, but at the same time it has a unique mood and feeling of its own - a strange, science-fiction kind of funk which infuses the sound. Tellingly, Alcantara was a New York resident and to me this album feels like something that could only have been dreamed up in 1970's Manhattan. It's not the aristocratic prog-rock of England but a melting pot of influences, drawing from the sound of the Manhattan nightclubs, the city's high profile avant-garde scene and the various global cultures which were then active on the island.

In fact *Zygoat* walks a peculiar line between the warm analogue electronic music heard at places like the loft parties of David Mancuso and the wilder side of the fine arts. It's a world away from the Berlin school of electronic sound in 1974, and seems oddly both more refined and simultaneously more acid-fried. It may not be as focussed on space as so many of the other records listed here but it is definitely stranger.

This is one of those albums that will appeal to a wide range of people: prog rock fans will love the fusion of composition and wigged out keyboards, experimental music fans will fall for its uniqueness, Balearic music fans will welcome the blissed out electronic baroque soul music feeling. It's a secret joy.

Second hand copies do seem to be fairly well available online. It does have some quiet, blissful passages so I would recommend making sure the vinyl is at least VG+ condition - and the sleeve is so lovely you really want that in the same condition.

PADDY KINGSLAND – SUPERCHARGED
Label: Studio to Stereo
ID: TWOX 1024

Tracklist
A1 - Money, Money, Money
A2 - Cecilia
A3 - Gollum

A4 - Autumn Dream
A5 - Wobulator Rock
A6 - The Wombling Song
B1 - Get Back
B2 - Killing Me Softly With His Song
B3 - The Earthmen
B4 - Top of The World
B5 - Fillet of Soul
B6 – Splashdown

Supercharged (released as *Supercharged Moog* in Australia) is that rare thing – an album that is simultaneously both ridiculously over the top and yet irresistibly joyous. Recorded at Abbey Road for EMI as a stereo demonstration, it sounds big, loud, raucous and ambitious while at the same time being cheeky, cheery and frankly quite silly. The moog is the dominant instrument here but backed up by drums, guitars, strings, brass – the full works. 'Gollum', for instance, could be a bit of very well-played pub rock if you removed the domineering electronic growler but with Kingsland at the top of the mix it becomes a TV quiz show theme par excellence.

There is a definite sense of humour at work on this album, as Kingsland records a version of the music from children's TV favourites The Wombles but lovingly rendered in headphone-blowing arrangements as dense and complex as anything The Beatles ever committed to tape. Speaking of The Beatles, there's also a cover of 'Get Back' that swaps Macca for a moog and adds some righteous brass and funky vocoder. The cover of 'Killing

Me Softly with His Song' is pretty audacious and slides right along the razor edge of ridiculousness, but with this formidable team of musicians on his side, Kingsland pulls it off magnificently. Beautiful violins, a slow and sweet soul beat, not to mention an injection of pedal steel guitar combine to make the whole an aural treat.

'The Earthmen' is a particular jaw-dropper and is the track most likely to crop up on compilations. With a genuinely funky and dramatic sound, it's probably the best movie theme that never was (unless Tarantino ever hears it!)

It's not all roses, though; the version of The Carpenters 'Top of the World' really doesn't need to exist. It attempts subtlety but this is not a subtle record, making it the runt of the litter.

To an uninformed person browsing old records this could look like just another rubbish cheesy easy listening covers album but is actually mind-blowing in places. If you're looking for the Valhalla of electronic funky pop music then steer your velvet longships over here. As some of the songs on here work excellently in an exotic DJ set, the price for this one is unlikely to go below £20 for a copy that plays well. Of course, it's all so loud that a little bit of surface noise is seriously going to be drowned out.

PADDY KINGSLAND – SPINBALL
Label: EMI
ID: 2110

Tracklist
A1 - Spinball (Theme from *Rugby Special*)
B1 - Wobulator Rock

A bit of a puzzle this one. It's described as the theme to *Rugby Special* but everyone seems to remember a different song - 'Holy Mackerel' by Brian Bennett – as the *Rugby Special* theme. I'm sure hanging around vintage TV discussion forums could shed some light on this but mental health and safety laws forbid me to endorse such suggestions. Probably best just not to worry about it...

'Spinball's stomping drumming with upfront keyboard melodies resembles a rock song turned synthesiser piece. While it may not have made much of an impression on rugby fans, it certainly did on American jazz musician Herbie Mann who covered it on his 1974 album *London Underground* alongside songs by the Rolling Stones, the Beatles, Donovan and Traffic.

This recording is undoubtedly from the same sessions as *Supercharged* and I am sure when that album finally makes it to CD this will be a bonus track. Until that time however this 7" (backed by the wonderful 'Wobulator Rock') is the only place you will find it but it is worth the effort (I know I'm bad influence, but it is!).

PADDY KINGSLAND - WOBULATOR ROCK
Label: EMI
ID: EMI 2398

Tracklist
A - Wobulator Rock
B - Get Back

A nice little promo-only single, nothing exclusive but very handy for DJs. 'Wobulator Rock' is such a grand and groovy number that it can make a nice oddity in any DJ set. A Beatles cover for the b-side is a little obvious but it's such an engaging and boisterous arrangement that it can bring a smile to the hardest hearts.

DAVE SNELL - PLAYS THE HITS ON THE HARP
Label: BBC
ID: EMI 2398

(re-issued as 'The Harp in Harmony' on BBC Records in 1978, REC 311)

Tracklist
A1 - You are the Sunshine of My Life
A2 - Top of the World
A3 - Guitar Man
A4 - Cloud 7
A5 - Windmills of Your Mind
A6 - Tie a Yellow Ribbon

B1 - I Saw the Light
B2 - Mrs. Robinson
B3 - Killing Me Softly With His Song
B4 - Valley's End
B5 - We've Only Just Begun
B6 - My Cherie Amour

The incredulous reader may be scratching their head at the inclusion of this one but whilst a little quaint, it does credit Paddy Kingsland on synthesizer and so it counts! Even so, it may look a little out of place but bear with me.

For this album, Mr. Snell and his harp replace the lead vocal parts of popular songs of the era, accompanied by a backing band playing groovy, mellow rhythms, kicking off with a very laid back take on Stevie Wonder's 'You are the Sunshine Of My Life'. Sure, you *could* call it easy listening but it isn't cheesy and is done with a lot of flair.

Aside from the covers, there are a couple of rather fine original compositions, including the sublime 'Cloud 7' where I can detect a bit of synth adding some able support. However it's not Kingsland breaking out and playing distinctively, rather he's adding a subtle layer to a complex composition (and like everything on this album, the song is all about the harp with everything else below it in the mix). The only other place I detected Kingsland was on the wonderfully psychedelic outro to Todd Rundgren's 'I Saw the Light'.

They are all wonderful arrangements and even if you find any of the original songs annoying, you should be fine with these versions. I have always felt a little queasy about The Carpenters but Snell makes them palatable. He's better known to modern audiences as David Snell and just four years later the Beeb reissued this record as *Harp in Harmony* and credited him that way. Still, it's not uncommon to find the first version sold online under the David moniker.

Snell also worked with orchestras, jazz bands and recorded for nearly every major music library. His work was rediscovered by another generation as it found his way onto one of the Sound Gallery compilations and on a mix album from Thievery Corporation. He's not messing about, in other words, he really is a harp master and this is a fun, pleasant and mildly funky little album.

1975

BBC RADIOPHONIC WORKSHOP - THE RADIOPHONIC WORKSHOP
Label: BBC Records
ID: REC196

Tracklist
A1.1–La Grande Pièce De La Foire De La Rue Delaware (Malcolm Clarke)
A1.2–Brio (John Baker)
A2 – Adagio (Dick Mills)
A3 – Geraldine (Roger Limb)
A4 – Bath Time (Malcolm Clarke)

A5 – Nénuphar (Glynis Jones & Malcolm Clarke)
B1.1–Major Bloodnok's Stomach (Dick Mills)
B1.2–The Panel Beaters (Paddy Kingsland)
B1.3–Crazy Dazy (Dick Mills)
B2 – Veils and Mirrors (Glynis Jones)
B3 – Romanescan Rout (Malcolm Clarke)
B4 – Schlum Rooli (Glynis Jones)
B5 – Kitten's Lullaby (Roger Limb)
B6 – Waltz Antipathy (Richard Yeoman - Clark)
B7 – The World of Science (Paddy Kingsland)

Whilst 1968's celebrated 'pink album' was actually a compilation of work commissioned for radio and television, this follow up compilation from 1975 is almost entirely brand new music, created especially for this LP. For obvious titular reasons, the two albums are always paired up but given that the '68 album compiled existing work, and nearly ten years separate them, it does neither title any favours.

Malcolm Clarke seizes the chance to break free immediately with the brash opening track 'La Grande Pièce de la Foire de la Rue Delaware', an overwhelmingly loud carnival waltz blasted out on the Delaware synth with a little help from Richard Yeoman-Clarke. It's rambunctious fun with a heavy low end and ably sets the tone for the remainder of the album.

John Baker is the only survivor from the Pink album's line-up and his contribution, 'Brio', is one of his wonderful funky tracks with a very weird arrangement

Dick Mills gets very spooky on 'Adagio', a piece that brings to mind the unearthly background sounds he made for alien worlds on *Doctor Who* though it would need to be for something far darker than BBC1 teatime would allow.

All of which makes the easy listening melodies of Roger Limb's 'Geraldine' leap out in aural technicolour straight afterwards. Reminiscent of Ennio Morricone's lighter 1970's work but created electronically, this change of pace is very welcome and demonstrates the sheer range of Workshop output very effectively.

Malcolm Clarke returns with the beautiful, misty-eyed 'Bath Time' which conjures up jazz musician Raymond Scott's electronic work for babies and gives them a good, melodic '70s polish, a world away from the Clarke's wild opening and hard to conceive as the work of the same man.

Next, Clarke follows himself, in collaboration with Glynis Jones, on 'Nénuphar' which may be named after a water lily but sounds more like dead wind echoing through a ruined city while the only survivors, the machines, try to drown it out with their own simple melodies. It's an eerie ending for side one of the LP, leaving the listener discomfited and uneasy.

This creepy atmosphere promptly gets obliterated as you flip the record over and are hit with Dick Mill's old sound effect for the comedy ensemble, The Goons' 'Major Bloodnok's Stomach' which segues without pause into Paddy Kingsland's bright and jaunty 'The Panel Beaters' with its big, loud synth sound and happy melodies. After a brief pause we get 'Crazy Dazy' which sounds like a distorted field recording of a peaceful meadow and 'Daisy, Daisy' played on a bicycle bell before a car crashes into the meadow and the familiar song continues on its manipulated bell. It really is as bonkers as it sounds.

Everything changes, when Glynis Jones reappears on her own to do 'Veils and Mirrors', an eerie piece that would have been perfect for a '70s European horror film and which leaves you wishing there were more Glynis Jones releases out there.

Malcolm Clarke next presents 'Romanescan Rout', a symphony of sound with more layers than I can count and a growling bass line that on the right hi-fi system seems to come close to the mythical brown note. The final Glynis Jones track 'Schlum Rooli' features distorted echoes of children singing and a strange keyboard melody. Not one to listen to on your own in an old house.

A more sedate mood is restored by Roger Limb's 'Kitten's Lullaby' which makes me think less of kittens and more of a very posh restaurant somewhere in the future. Richard Yeoman Clarke's 'Waltz Antipathy' is very odd – the title sort of says it all, as it is a waltz fed through an electronic blender which begins to distort more and more into almost noise music.

It all ends with Paddy Kingsland's 'The World of Science' with its cheerful air of normality easing you gently back to real life with a tapping toe.

It wouldn't be an exaggeration to call this the compulsory Radiophonic Workshop purchase.

The BBC reissued the album on CD in 2002 with a lovely remaster and two bonus John Baker tracks – the uncharacteristic 'Accentric' which is quite a dark piece of Oriental-influenced minimalism with an understated techno rhythm and the similarly sparse and rhythmic 'Chino'. Mute Records then reissued this reissue in 2008 on their Grey Area label for experimental music, so with a little work you should be able to get the CD for a normal price. Meanwhile, vinyl lovers should have no problems as Music On Vinyl reissued the album in 2013. Everything on here and the Pink album, including bonus tracks, was featured on Rephlex's compilation 'Music from the BBC Radiophonic Workshop'. So, there's no excuse for not having these wonderful sounds in your collection.

THE WHITE NOISE - WHITE NOISE 2 CONCERTO FOR SYNTHESIZER
Label: Virgin Records
ID: V2032

Tracklist
A1 – Movement I
A2 – Movement II
B1 – Movement II (continued)
B2 – Movement III

First things first, I have to make it very clear that is absolutely nothing like its famous predecessor. There are no vocals, no wonky pop, no Delia or Brian or anything you would associate with the first album. It does what it says on the cover - it's a classical-inspired composition for the synthesiser. Even forearmed with this knowledge, the first listen does come as a disappointment. It's still a good album but it's not the timeless classic that the first album is. Perhaps had it been released here as it was in Japan -as simply David Vorhaus' 'Concerto For Synthesizer' - then its legacy might be more positive but then The White Noise always was Vorhaus' baby and why should he change his recording name?

It is split into three movements, with the second being divided between the two sides of vinyl (and appears as two distinct tracks on the CD reissue). The first movement is the most baroque contain some wild proggy moments of electronic classical excess as well as some mad moments of sound manipulation. The best bit is the second movement with its dark moody minimalism. It definitely feels like a precursor both to dark ambient and to those mid 90s Warp Records that took techno out of the club and turned it into a home listening experience, people like Black Dog and Beaumont Hannant.

The third movement goes for all out epic climax, with a drummer suddenly added to the music, starting off in full on dramatic drum rolls. One of the biggest problems with this album is its context. By 1975 albums of synthesizer music were very common. The first and third movements are nothing particularly different to contemporary synth albums. It is all in the second movement where it gets interesting. Make no mistake, it is still an enjoyable album, just not one that will make the classic album lists. You just have to accept the album on its own terms.

WAVEMAKER – WHERE ARE WE CAPTAIN?
Label: Polydor
ID: 2383 331

Tracklist
A1 - Lodestar
A2 – Double Helix
A3 – Syren's Song
B1 – Wavemaker
B2 – Oracle
B3 – Enter the Eldil

The duo of John Lewis and Brian Hodgson as Wavemaker has long remained an obscure footnote in music. Their two vinyl-only albums for Polydor seem to have passed by most listeners, with only prog rock enthusiasts picking it up – and even they appear to have found themselves a little bit bemused at times.

It's not hard to see why. Whilst Lewis was classically trained, he seemed to have no aptitude for the pomp and bluster required by contemporary progressive rock. His work with Hodgson at Electrophon as Wavemaker shows a thoughtful, intuitive musician exploring the melodic possibilities of synthesisers. The Hawkwind-esque record cover misleads the listener because there really isn't anything else around like this, least of all Dave Brock and Co. It's not drug music, space worship or chaotic improvisation- this is the John Lewis who went on to record 'Pop Muzik' as part of M, after all.

Instead, it's an edgy but tuneful album, enhanced by a percussionist and a timpani player whose rhythmic backbeat propels along the rather congenial electronics. You can't call it a chill-out album, as some of the percussion is quite loud and dramatic, while several of the synth break downs are equally noisy. It's almost impossible to categorise, in fact, beyond noting that it's a 'synth album', but even that generic label doesn't quite work, as Wavemaker doesn't belong next to, say. Klaus Schulze and Tangerine Dream in your record collection.

Perhaps it's this refusal to fall into a simple category that makes Wavemaker such a difficult album to pin down. It's melodic but not sedate; it's made with space age synths but doesn't sound remotely spacey; it was made in the '70s but has a sound that does not belong to any time.

"Where are we Captain?" asks the title. I don't know but it seems like a charming, amiable place.

BRIAN HODGSON AND JOHN LEWIS – ENCORE ELECTRONIC
Label: Standard Music Library
ID: ESL133

Tracklist
A1 - Arcadian Valley
A2 - Grotto
A3 - Nerve Centre
A4 - Galactic Clock

A5 - Crystal Forms
A6 - Interstellar Chatter
A7 - Astro Monitor
A8 - Quasar
A9 - Quasar Link I
A10 - Quasar Link II
A11 - Cosmic Cloud
A12 - The Craters Of Mars
A13 - Dimensional Drift
B1 - Logo Rhythmic 1A
B2 - Logo Rhythmic 1B
B3 - Logo Rhythmic II
B4 - Logo Rhythmic III
B5 - Logo Rhythmic IV
B6 - Logo Rhythmic V
B7 - Logo Rhythmic VI
B8 - Interlude
B9 - Cathedral Of Space
B10 - Winds Of The Void
B11 - Happy Machine
B12 - Song Of The Wilderness
B13 - Caverns Of The Deep
B14 - Random Purpose
B15 - Stratonimbus
B16 - After The Rains
B17 - Banshee
B18 - Programmadate
B19 - Startide
B20 - Dance Of The Virus

Freed from BBC contracts and running his own Electrophon studio, Brian Hodgson was able to use his real name for this album of library music for the Standard Music Library. In fact, although credited to Hodgson and his Wavemaker/Electrophon partner John Lewis, they only actually collaborate on five of the thirty three tracks on here, with the remainder being credited to one or the other. I don't know about you but before I heard this album I knew I was in for a treat. I hate to speak so highly of an album that's a pain in the arse to get hold of but it's a gem.

Encore Electronic is packed full of odd, atmospheric, melodic but eccentric electronics. Having only recently discovered it, I have yet to find out where it has been used but I can see how it would be a gold mine for anyone making sci-fi or arthouse films. John Lewis in particular makes some very intense, proto-acid wig outs., while Hodgson on the other hand makes music more akin to *musique concrète* filtered through 60s decadence to create something as beautiful as it is bizarre. Evocative titles like 'Cathedral of Space', 'Happy Machine' and 'Winds of The Void' make good on their promise and deliver new worlds in crisp stereo electronic sound.

This LP is so effortlessly charming that you would have to be a disagreeable sort to not get on with it. Frustratingly, this one has never been reissued in any form so at the time of writing only the original LP from 1975 is available, and you'll struggle to find a copy in enjoyable condition for under £50. However, given the quality of it, a reissue is as inevitable as rain in an English summer so if you don't fancy paying more for an LP than a flight to Europe then just bide your time because the good will always out.

1976

BBC RADIOPHONIC WORKSHOP - OUT OF THIS WORLD
Label: BBC Records and Tapes
ID: REC225

Tracklist

Outer Space

Sea Of Mercury
Galactic Travel
Tardis Take-Off
Tardis Land
Space Rocket Take-Off
Space Rocket Land
Flying Saucer Land
Flying Saucer Take-Off
Flying Saucer Interior Constant Run
Space Ship Control Room Atmosphere
Space Ship Interior Atmosphere
Electric Door Open
Electric Door Shut
Laser Gun, Five Bursts

"Computer"
Gravity Generator
Time Warp Start, Run, Stop
Venusian Space Lab.
Andromeda War Machine
Space-battle

Magic and Fantasy

Dance of Fire-Flies
Dreaming
Crystal City
Enchanted Forest
Goblins Lair
Magic Carpet Take-Off
Magic Carpet Flight
Magic Carpet Land
Magic Flower Grows and Buds
Magic Beanstalk Grows
Star Fairies
Midsummer Elves
Fairy Appears
Fairy Disappears
Wizard Flies Off
Casting A Spell
Magic Mushroom
Magic Bird Song

Suspense And The Supernatural

Phantoms of Darkness
Uncanny Expectation
Spectres in The Wind
Evil Rises Up
Threatening Shadow
Moments of Terror
Passing Shade
Psychic Fears
Two Terror Twangs
Three Terror Bangs
Terror Zing
Terror Glissando
"Thing" Approaches
Roaring Monster
Firespitting Monster
Nightmare Forest
Fiendish Shrieks

The Elements

Heat Haze
Desert Sands
Frozen Waste
Icy Peak
Snow Swirls
Passing Clouds
Starry Skies
Electric Storm

Watery Depths
Rising Bubbles
Spring Tide

Rarely out of print, this compilation features a dream team line-up of John Baker, David Cain, Delia Derbyshire, Brian Hodgson, Peter Howell, Malcolm Clarke, Glynis Jones (who also compiled this record), Paddy Kingsland, Roger Limb, Dick Mills and Richard Yeoman Clark. Not until the 2008's *Retrospective* was there a bigger line-up of Radiophonic talent. The only issue here is that *Out of this World* is a compilation of sound effects and atmospheres for amateur dramatic productions to use. It wasn't initially conceived as a home listening LP, although it is regularly enjoyed as one.

Jones gathered together lots of small pieces from the Workshop (multiple contributions from all bar Yeoman-Clark & Kingsland) and arranging them into the themes of 'Outer Space', 'Magic and Fantasy', 'Suspense and The Supernatural' and 'The Elements', but if truth be told, it all sounds pretty Outer Space to me. Also, the rapid fire nature of the tracks means that four or five tracks into each side, you soon lose track of which one you are actually listening too, preventing you from getting any sense of whose work it is.

It is, however, still wonderful and a great album to chill out to. Prince seems to have agreed and used one of Roger Limb's tracks on here as the intro to his album *Lovesexy*. It's all pleasingly futuristic if not a genuine

Radiophonic classic but still a relevant part of the discography.

SWAG - SWAG
Label: EMI
ID: EMC 3135

Tracklist
A1 - Love Dance
A2 - Tow the Line
A3 - In the Bag
A4 - London
A5 - Jumpin' Off the Bandwagon
A6 - Can't Stop Loving You
B1 - Keep on Holding On
B2 - Quacky
B3 - Turn Around
B4 - Sweet Blossom
B5 - Kippers (The Secret of The Universe)
B6 - Time to Say Goodbye

If, like me, you come to the Swag album quite late in your obsessive Radiophonic-related record collecting, then you're in for a bit of a surprise. For the duo of Paddy Kingsland and Richard Bellevue-de Sylva (better known for producing folk music such as Bonnie Dobson) will take your Workshop collection to places it's never been before. Opening track 'Love Dance' doesn't seem too unusual at first, with a nice back beat and some typically Kingsland squelchy keyboards doing cheeky melodies - but then a soul singer arrives, complete with female backing singers urging 'come on baby, do the love dance'. The year is 1976, the place is Abbey Road Studios and it seems the influence of disco, soul and funky was high in the air. A simple song like 'London' has breezy Bacharach meets Salsoul strings, a bouncing beat and zoned out keyboards.

It's not all soul and disco, though; there's the curious 'Jumpin' off the Bandwagon' which attempts the reggae/country hybrid the world didn't know it wanted. I once dropped it in a DJ set by mistake after a few too many pints of blonde ale and the audience looked a bit puzzled. Meanwhile, 'Quacky' sounds a lot like something from 'Moogerama', totally focussed on those big, loud keyboard sounds with a subtle backing behind.

However, on something like 'Turn Around', the rhythm section really comes to the fore and it could easily sit in a basement soul music DJ set. There's also a track called 'Sweet Blossom' that doesn't have any groove at all and serves instead as a bit of easy listening. The toughest, funkiest track though is the amusingly named 'Kippers (the secret of the universe)' with its gritty horn section, wah-wah and right on rhythms.

It probably helps if you have had your hand in the disco biscuits cookie jar at some point in your life but there's no denying the strange charm of this Swag record and its singular place in the Radiophonic Workshop-affiliated discography.

As yet, there has been no cd reissue of Swag, but if ever a record was ready to make its debut on shiny disc, this is the one.

1977

WAVEMAKER – NEW ATLANTIS
Label: Polydor
ID: 2383434

Tracklist
A1 - Salomon's House
A2 - The Pool
A3 - Merchants Of Light
A4 - Waters Of Paradise
Echoes Suite ("We Also Have Sound Houses...")
B1 - Echoes A
B2 - Echoes B
B3 - Echoes C
B4 - Towers And Caves

The return of Hodgson and Lewis accompanied by their faithful percussionist/wildman drummer Tony McVey is an album dedicated to Sir Francis Bacon's eerily prophetic essay of the same name. Given that provenance, it's no huge shock that *New Atlantis* certainly sounds to me like the more inspirational and experimental of the two albums.

Opening track 'Solomon's House' sets the scene perfectly for this more romantic, introspective sort of an album. Kicking off with some synth noodling which wouldn't be out of place in a 1970s UK science-fiction series, McVey's makes an appearance at the minute and a half mark, with drumming which is a almost contradiction in terms, a strangely gentle display of power, shoring up the swooping electronic sounds and providing them with a solid anchor.

McVey's work is merely one of many contradictions about this album. It's melodic but not pop, strange but not trippy, classical music with keyboards and drums but not prog, unabrasive but not relaxing. In fact it's impossible to talk about this album without rambling. It's an evasively singular album to try and discuss.

It is, simply, a thing of distinctive beauty. Like all the Electrophon albums the sound quality is first rate with the notes positively exploding off the vinyl through your speakers. When someone finally gets round to putting out these records as CD reissues, they will have to pay for some expert remastering to try and match the vivid sound of these vinyls. After this album, the only further release by Wavemaker was a 7" from 1977 called 'Tunnel of Love' (Polydor, 2058 924) which Lewis co-wrote with someone called Ben Cross and which would seem to be after Brian Hodgson went back to the Workshop. It's hard to imagine the chemistry being *quite* the same with a different lineup.

1978

BBC RADIOPHONIC WORKSHOP - DR WHO SOUND EFFECTS NO.19
Label: BBC Records and Tapes
ID: REC316

Not the nineteenth volume of *Doctor Who* sound effects but a special Doctor Who themed nineteenth volume of the BBC's sound effects series. Barring four TARDIS sounds and a sonic screwdriver noise from Brian Hodgson, this 1978 album is all Dick Mills special sounds. Side one is easily the best, as it contains eight long textured atmospheric background pieces which, although not commissioned as incidental music at the time, by contemporary standards that's clearly what they are. Strange, ethereal evocations of alien worlds.

Side two begins on a similar note with more extended scenic pieces but then, after the brief suite of Hodgson sounds, you get nine different laser gun effects. While that is not unreasonable given that this whole release was conceived for amateur dramatists to use as sound effects, it does bugger with the modern listening experience, creating a disappointing finale to what had up till then been an exemplary album of experimental electronic music.

There is no middle ground here, casuals are definitely not welcome. To appreciate this album you either have to be a hardcore *Doctor Who* fan or a lover of ambient drones. You are not whacking this one on when the in-laws pop round for tea, basically (unless you have particularly cool in-laws!)

The vinyl is easy to obtain, having had a few recent reissues, including a Record Store Day blue vinyl which still goes for an affordable amount. However, CD versions have been a bit thinner on the ground with a 1990 release (hardly a great time for digital remastering) and then a 2012 release on the now defunct AudioGO label.

BBC RADIOPHONIC WORKSHOP/PETER HOWELL - THROUGH A GLASS DARKLY
Label: BBC Records
ID: REC317

Tracklist
A1 - Through A Glass Darkly - A Lyrical Adventure
B1 - Caches of Gold
B2 - Magenta Court
B3 - Colour Rinse
B4 - Wind in The Wires
B5 - The Astronauts

The first proper artist-led Radiophonic Workshop album since 1968's *The Seasons* sees Peter Howell create a wonderful space age synth-prog album, calling in a few chums from his old band days to work this as a band ensemble.

Beginning with the epic twenty minute title track which takes up the whole of side one, it manages to avoid the pomp and noodling of the times, moving from sweepingly lyrical keyboards to classical piano and back again. Howell plays sublime piano all the way across the intro, in fact, and then gives way to some wonderful synth work which sounds like the warbling of stars. The listener can feel space rushing towards him at high speed before a sudden stillness in which a single soft drum like a heartbeat dominates, before the piano comes back, as charming as you like. Compare this to what Tangerine Dream were doing in 1978 and Howell comes up trumps with something far more restrained and interesting than the gloopy excesses of *Cyclone*.

Side two is five more normal length tracks. The first two tracks are quite rocking with stomping rhythms and chugging guitars and synths, almost like Deep Purple at the Radiophonic Workshop. Then the third song, 'Colour Rises' suddenly changes tone completely sounding like the intro to a fun TV show. Following that is 'Wind in the Wires' where psychedelic folk guitars mix with pastoral synths. From nowhere, it seems, we witness the return of the Peter Howell of Agincourt and Ithaca, restored to life in the Radiophonic Workshop. The final track, the epic 'The Astronauts' - originally created for a BBC documentary debunking Erich von Däniken[96] - is now justly a part of the live Radiophonic Workshop's sets. After a suitably teasing cosmic intro, 'The Astronauts' builds up into a breath-taking epic synth space theme. A fittingly climactic ending to the album.

At the time of writing, *Through A Glass Darkly* has just been given an audiophile vinyl reissue by Dutch label Music On Vinyl, but no CD version has appeared as yet, and one track appears on the *A Retrospective* compilation, for which the remastering does not manage to fully preserve the warm magic of the vinyl version. A sad state of affairs, although there is something apt about the charms of this album being reserved for those discerning souls who still buy vinyl and denied to the CD and mp3 crowd.

PADDY KINGSLAND - MOOGERAMA
Label: Amphonic Music Limited
ID: AMPS 121

Tracklist
A1 Wheel To Wheel
A2 Night Watch
A3 March of The Moogs
A4 Wobble in Time
A5 When Love Has Gone
A6 Electric Hustle
B1 Space Race
B2 Puffing Billy
B3 Green Serene
B4 Tearaway
B5 January's Child
B6 Night on The Town

This album could be the cousin of *Supercharged*. Once again it sees Paddy Kingsland team up with a backing group in a big studio, but this time the emphasis is on original material with a broad scope.

The opening track 'Wheel To Wheel' is a full-on cheeky stomper but is followed by the dark and mysterious 'Night Watch', which sounds like the theme tune to a TV crime series set in some distant European city complete with some wonderful brass parts.

'March of the Moogs' starts off a bit too saccharine with a melody too corny to be stomached outside of a nursery rhyme and with accompanying military drums, but midway through a sudden funky breakdown intrudes that makes you glad you didn't stop listening.

One thing about Kingsland is that he is one of the few people to use a vocoder and not make me want to throw rocks at them. On 'Wobble In Time' he uses it so well you forgive the instrument all the obscenities it has foisted upon us over the years.

Most of the songs on here have their virtues but after the first few tracks the album runs out of steam quite drastically. The main issue is it is far too middle of the road. Plenty of the easy listening albums Kingsland was involved with had such strong jazz roots that you could pluck some of them out for an eclectic DJ set, but nothing on *Moogerama* really breaks out in the way that, for example, 'Wobulator Rock' did on the previous album.

The closest would be 'Tearaway' which resembles an Elton John song with his vocals taken off and an unsatisfying moog melody quickly substituted. In similar vein, 'Space Race' with its loud flashes of high camp disco funk, almost hits the mark apart from during the breakdown, but never quite hits the heights.

It's not a bad album and it never offends the listener, while its place in Radiophonic history endears it and there is certain quaintness to the arrangements that appeals, but it is in no way a worthy follow up to the mighty *Supercharged*. Paddy Kingsland had many times proven his enormous talent which is what makes this average album feel like a missed opportunity, particularly as he clearly has some fantastic musicians accompanying him.

SAILOR: A PICTURE IN SOUND OF THE ROYAL NAVY
Label: BBC Records
ID: REH318

Tracklist
A1 –Morning Departure / Warship
A2 –Fog / Neptune, The Mystic
A3 – Missile / Veni Creatur Spiritus
A4 –Divine Service / Western Approaches
A5 –Torpedo / In Her Majesty's Secret Service
A6 –Run Ashore / Theme from Zorba The Greek - Who Plays The Ferryman?
B1 – Requiem / Adagio
B2 – Flying Stations /Fly Robin Fly
B3 – Northern Flank / When Eagles Dare

B4 – Gale Force / Theme One
B5 – Coming Home / Sailing
B6 - Night on The Town

This BBC compilation takes us back to the golden age of vinyl, when new records were not a luxury item for devoted music obsessives but an everyday item for people from all walks of life. This LP is a curious tribute to the Royal Navy through blended music and sound put together by Mike Harding, who produced all the BBC sound effects records.

It's a compilation of existing music, mostly classical, all with sound recordings of life in the Royal Navy superimposed over the top. For instance, the album opens with The Band of H.M. Royal Marines performing 'Warship' whilst dubbed over it are officers conducting the vessel's departure. You also get to hear the Monastic Choir of Hauterive Abbey, Switzerland performing 'Veni Creator Spiritus' whilst commands are given for launching a missile at enemy targets. Perhaps most bizarrely, the 'Theme from Zorba The Greek' is played at the end of side one and accompanied by the sound of a lads night out during shore leave, including drunken singing of 'Land of Hope and Glory' and someone being told off for not having any trousers on.

So, how is it Radiophonic? Well, in a genius move, side two opens with Dick Mill's haunting classic 'Adagio' while a narrator reads out an account of the burial of the poet Sub Lieutenant Rupert Brook, RNVR. Of course, 'Adagio' is on the second Radiophonic Workshop compilation and extended on the *Relaxing Sounds* compilation (also produced by Harding). It works beautifully and makes another nice alternative version of an already great piece of music.

Following on from it we get Silver Convention's disco rock track 'Fly Robin-Fly', accompanied by some aircraft taking off and doing missions. Ending with the Ship's Company and Band of HMS Ark Royal singing 'Sailing', this is one of those albums that is far better than it sounds on paper and you will find yourself listening to it all the way through, not just to the Dick Mills track, because the music is so well chosen, and the Naval sound effects make it unique. If you find this in the charity shop, second hand market or jumble sale then please don't hesitate.

1979

BBC RADIOPHONIC WORKSHOP - 21
Label: *BBC Records*
ID: *REC 354*

To celebrate the Workshop's 21st birthday, this fabulous compilation was put together by Brian Hodgson and Roger Limb. A rather choice selection and smartly arranged, side one is entirely in mono and features many of Delia Derbyshire's most pivotal works, alongside a brace of John Baker tunes and some early gems from Desmond Briscoe, Phil Young and Maddalena Fagandini. There's the TARDIS take-off from *Doctor Who*, and the original 'Time Beat' before George Martin got his hands on it and everything arranged in chronological order so that the listener get a sense of how things changed between 1958 (the earliest work here) and 1971 (the last track on side one).

Kicking off with a little bit of *Quatermass and the Pit* and then the sound of Major Bloodnok's tortured digestive tract, it's strange to think of these as sounds of the 1950s. The earlier work is more simple and textured but once Delia Derbyshire and John Baker arrive on the scene, the same work methods begin to sound more intensely intricate and complex. On 'Great Zoos of the World' Derbyshire makes a whole multi-tracked tune out of animal noises - a relatively straight-forward task with today's technology but in the 1960s it must have taken her literally days to create. Her 1963 'Know Your Car' theme manages to be melodic, car-like and verging on proto-funky techno. John Baker's empty bottle symphony for 'Choice' is simply a breathtaking 36 seconds of wonder. The gold never stops.

Side two is in stereo and is all considered recent work, designed to showcase the technological evolution of the Workshop. Here the classic 70s work of Paddy Kingsland, Malcolm Clarke, Peter Howell and Roger Limb dominate the landscape. Opening with the futuristic utopian 'Fanfare' by Dick Mills, it sets the scene for a very broad range of commissions that take on everything from children's comedy to music for religious programmes and serious documentaries.

The common myth that the '70s was the end of the

Workshop's creative life is disproven here as the quality seems to flow naturally from side one without any great disruption. The ever changing methods across side one make the shift to synthesizers seem completely natural. The almost spiritual uplift of Peter Howell's 'The Body In Question', and Malcolm Clarke paying tribute to the hurdy gurdy on the giant Synthi 100 is a surreal concept that works really well, sounding like a time travelling medieval musician let loose on the synth. Paddy Kinsgland's 'A Whisper from Space' really is perfectly named. I could go on and on but, like side one, the highlights are too numerous.

Although never released on CD, every single track on here is included in the 'Retrospective' compilation, although fitted into chronological order alongside many other things. Yet despite having it all on that release, there is something very compelling about both the track list and the fidelity of this release. Something that has me returning to it again and again. Its shorter running time makes it easier to fit into day to day listening and the sounds contained on it really do belong on vinyl.

RELAXING SOUNDS - SOUND EFFECTS VOL.23
Label: BBC Records
ID: REC 360

Tracklist
Country Stream (Lloyd Silverthorne)
Aerial Currents (Roger Limb)

A Garden in Springtime (Lloyd Silverthorne)
Seashore (Lloyd Silverthorne)
Forest Adagio (Dick Mills)
Rain (Lloyd Silverthorne)

Fancying a change after doing sound effect LPs of death, horror and disaster, the series producer Mike Harding (not the comedian) decided to try something very different. Of the six tracks on here, four are field recordings by Lloyds Silverthorne (who himself had previously served a placement at the Radiophonic Workshop) and the other two tracks from the Workshop itself.

Opening up with over seven minutes of a country stream in stereo, it really does what it says on the cover. Following from that is Roger Limb's 'Aerial Currents' which is a very ethereal and ambient piece originally created for radio programme *Icarus With An Oilcan* but lengthened and turned to stereo. I've not come across the original on any other release and at over seven minutes of futuristic bliss, it makes this LP a must for Radiophonic Workshop fans (when the price is right). After that, side one ends with a garden in springtime recorded in binaural sound (so on headphones it creates a surround sound effect).

Side two begins in binaural sound again with the sound of a seashore. I have never been one for natural sound releases but when they are around the seven minute mark and so well recorded, I do have to concede they have a certain charm. In any case, the second track is

'Forest Adagio' by Dick Mills - a new version of 'Adagio' from the second Workshop compilation, lasting a minute and a half longer. The sleeve notes claim the sounds of a West African tropical forest have been added but either I don't know what a West African tropical forest sounds like or it's not very obvious. Of course, it is a great track so to own the 'twelve inch version' is cool by me. The album ends with that old classic, the sound of rain.

With only two Workshop tracks, one of which was already widely released in a shorter form, the album might seem like a low priority but it is an oddly pleasing one that flows very well and genuinely does ease stress. Think of it was an EP or mini-album and at the right price it suddenly becomes an essential purchase.

1980

PETER HOWELL AND THE BBC RADIOPHONIC WORKSHOP – DOCTOR WHO THEME
Label: BBC Records
ID: BBC RESL80

Tracklist
A – Dr Who
B - Reg

The Peter Howell version of D*octor Who* theme tune was swiftly and proudly released as a single, complete with Tom Baker grinning lecherously on the cover (promptly reissued with Peter Davison smiling sweetly a year later). Such a bold re-imaging deserved the star treatment and the casuals were rewarded with 'The Astronauts' from Howell's earlier album 'Through a Glass Darkly' as the b-side. While you'd be pushed to describe these as long lost treasures, the humble seven inch was such an important part of music history that this release craves your indulgence. It looks and sounds lovely and should not set you back any more than a pint of beer in a city centre.

WHITE NOISE – III: RE-ENTRY
Label: Pulse Records
ID: PULSE 002

Tracklist
A1 - Countdown
A2 – Lift Off
A3 – Afterburn
A4 – Burn 2
A5 – Orbit
A6 – Leaving Song
A7 – Deep Space Drift
A8 – Meteor Storm
A9 – Disorientation
A10 – Time Traveller
B1 – Space Warp
B2 – Voices
B3 – Heavy Breathing
B4 – Black Hole Blues

B5 – Nine Dimensions
B6 – Nebulous meets Nebula
B7 – The Cygnus Constellation

1980 was a radical year for electronics. Throbbing Gristle released the wild and savage *Heathen Earth*, The Human League released *Travelogue* which refined their ideas of accessible electronic music with classics like 'Being Boiled', and Kraftwerk were putting the finishing touches to *Computer World*. It's at first a little hard to imagine that *Re-Entry* fits in with the electronica of this specific year. David Vorhaus has a resolutely futurist vision but by this point the young bucks were creating new futures and he was becoming one of the old guard. Yet, in reality, *Re-entry* does fit in with what was going on with electronic music in the 1980s.

Of course, it is a tribute to Vorhaus that this feels like such an eighties' album when it was only released in 1980. Using the same tools and sounds that would define a generation, Vorhaus seems determined to go his own way. The album is at first a little awkward and dated with its space concept and not quite successful attempts at pop music, but after the first ten minutes it finds its feet, and a niche of its own. The wilder more abstract stuff helps it distinguish itself and then the more groovy melodic stuff enters its own odd little world.

It is just a shame that the earlier parts of the album feel like an innovator trying to catch up and not succeeding, because they do make you consider switching off what is actually for the most part a very good album. In fairness, I'm not too sure about 'Black Hole Blues' which feels more like a Douglas Adams sketch than a work of music but otherwise it's pleasantly spacey. Even the bits that feel a bit clichéd only feel like clichés because so many others did the same thing afterward Vorhaus. Whilst *Re-Entry* couldn't be said to have seized the zeitgeist, it is a perfectly enjoyable album which improves as it goes along. Oh, and the album artwork is nothing short of stunning.

1981

BBC RADIOPHONIC WORKSHOP - SCIENCE FICTION SOUND EFFECTS NO.26
Label: BBC Records
ID: REC 420

Again with the confusing numbering.
This is the third compilation of BBC Radiophonic Workshop sound effects, which means that whilst the previous two albums were in the enviable position of cherry picking from well over a decade's worth of sound, this one attempts a more contemporary representation by presenting sound effects from four recent shows: *The Hitch-Hiker's Guide To The Galaxy* (radio version), the 1980 series of *Doctor Who*, Terry Nation's *Blakes 7* and a 1980 radio drama called *Earth Search*.
The track list is ordered by what programme they appeared in, rather than for any sort of listening continuity and whilst many of the effects are very

interesting, not as many of them transcend into actual listening pleasure as happened with the previous two sound effects compilations. Of course, allowances have to be as the first two LPs are 'best of' compilations while this is simply an album of the latest sounds from BBC television and radio shows. Which means that though every track is skilfully crafted and each is an essential embellishment of the drama that they were made for, there is not much to engage the home listener.

For the most part, the album simply glides by unremarkably. Of course, being a creation of the Workshop, there are sudden moments of genius that make you raise an eyebrow but for the most part, these are sound effects, no more and no less. If you want to make your own sci-fi radio play then you need this. If you're not then you don't. It feels almost dis-ingenious to be criticising a record for doing exactly what it says is does on the cover but that's just how it is!

VARIOUS ARTISTS – SPACE INVADED BBC SPACE THEMES
Label: BBC Records
ID: REH442

A lovely old compilation LP that kicks off with the Howell version of the *Doctor Who* theme, just in case you had any doubts about the calibre of music contained. No need to fear - it's almost all gold on here. Dudley Simpson's theme for *Blakes 7* in all its bluster, the very gentle and beautiful

Sibelius piece 'At The Castle Gate' as used for *The Sky At Night*, the bold and soaring sound Aaron Copland's 'Fanfare For The Common Man' (which the BBC had used for their coverage of the America space shuttle launch) and some very decent Vangelis music that was used for Carl Sagan's classic documentary *Cosmos*. All worthy tracks, deserving of multiple listens.

Side two starts well, with the very funky, cosmic disco style 1980 theme tune for *Tomorrow's World*, a piece way ahead of its time and at times almost flipping into techno. Unfortunately, we then get the theme from *Doctor Who* spin-off *K-9 And Company*, which sounds uncomfortably similar to the theme from *Garth Marenghi's Darkplace*. A lot of the blame for this theme gets thrown at co-composer Ian Levine but Peter Howell arranged it at the Radiophonic Workshop and must surely be accountable for some of the embarrassment caused by this awkward theme.

It's unfortunate, then, that after this unexpected dip in quality, the album attempts to divert your disturbed mind from that crime, with a horribly cheesy cover of the *Star Trek* theme by Charles Callelo featuring department store brass and pointless percussion.

Luckily next up is some of Peter Howell's excellent incidental music for *Doctor Who* serial 'The Leisure Hive' with its sprightly drums and euphoric synths providing a spectacular air of menace. Following this is Malcolm Clarke's 'The Comet Is Coming', a track that was not available anywhere else until the 2008 'Retrospective' compilation. It's a track of gentle synths with mad trumpet on top, of course it's a gem!

Ending this aural treat all is the theme from the TV version of *The Hitchiker's Guide To The Galaxy*, a cover by Tim Souster of the original radio theme, 'Journey Of The Sorcerer' by The Eagles.

1983

BBC RADIOPHONIC WORKSHOP – DOCTOR WHO THE MUSIC
Label: BBC Records
ID: BBC-22462 (LP)/ ZCR 462(cassette)

Tracklist
A1 – Tardis: Doctor Who (Ron Grainer)
A2 – The Sea Devils (Malcolm Clarke)
A3 – Meglos (Peter Howell)
A4 – Nyssa's Theme (Roger Limb)
A5 – Kassia's Wedding Music (Roger Limb)
A6 – The Threat of Melkur (Roger Limb)
A7 – Exploring the Lab (Roger Limb)
A8 – Nyssa Is Hypnotized (Roger Limb)
A9 – The Leisure Hive (Peter Howell)
B1 – Omega Field Force (Roger Limb)
B2 – Ergon Threat (Roger Limb)
B3 – Termination Of The Doctor (Roger Limb)
B4 – Banqueting Music (Peter Howell)
B5 – TSS Machine Attacked (Peter Howell)

B6 – Janissary Band
B7 – Subterranean Caves (Malcolm Clarke)
B8 – Requiem (Malcolm Clarke)
B9 – March Of The Cybermen (Malcolm Clarke)
B10 - Doctor Who (Ron Grainer)

Although the Radiophonic Workshop did all the sound effects for *Doctor Who*, their initial involvement in the incidental music was quite minimal. As a result, this compilation starts with the 1963 theme and Brian Hodgson's TARDIS sound then goes straight forward to a generous portion of Malcolm Clarke's wild score for 'The Sea Devils' from 1972 (with the harsh bits cut out, giving it more of a John Carpenter vibe) and then the next stop is as far forward as 1980, when the Workshop got the job of regularly doing soundtracks for the show. This century has seen the Workshop's *Doctor Who* soundtracks slowly being presented as individual albums with every single cue included. Here, though, we get a very different approach with a couple of serials represented by simple suites of incidental music whilst others get two three choice pieces presented for the listener's delight.

The gaps between pieces is very small making it feel almost like a mix album...and tricky to keep track of if you're listening on vinyl or cassette, even with an encyclopaedic memory of all things *Doctor Who*. So, in quick summary, side one continues with Peter Howell providing some dark growlings from 'Meglos' followed by Roger Limb delivering some sprightly wedding muzak and ominous corridor music from 'The Keeper Of Traken'. The side ends in style with some of Howell's finest incidental work for the series, the cloning of warriors from 'The Leisure Hive'.

Side two begins with high drama and an enormous amount of implied threat from Roger Limb's 'Arc Of Infinity' soundtrack. Limb doesn't mess about and creates a score like a 1980s sci-fi movie classic, and not a strange story about a giant chicken in a basement in Amsterdam preying on handsome young backpackers! I'm not too keen overall on Peter Howell's soundtrack for 'Warrior's Gate' but its represented here by the exception, the exquisite 'Banqueting Music', full of atmosphere and evocation of forgotten tragedy.

Brief passes of the un-nerving Howell soundtracks for 'Kinda' and its sequel 'Snakedance' follow, strange and tense pieces of strange ambience. The final serial featured is 'Earthshock', with its gregariously terrifying Malcolm Clarke soundtrack pumping out fear, threat and menace, yet also tragedy with its requiem for a mortally wounded trooper. The whole is topped off with a lap of victory for the Peter Howell version of the theme tune.

Released in 1983, it really sounds like the Workshop were the only ones who could have sound tracked *Doctor Who* at that point in time. With a few Dick Mills sound effects cleverly snuck in, it makes a nice, varied listen, covering a key era in the series' history. The compilation has been intelligently summarised and manages to make a suitable playlist while diligently retaining chronological order. Perhaps at some point every soundtrack featured on here will get a full and complete release, but this album has such a likeable running order that you would still find yourself returning to it even if you owned each individual score.

Cassette (*FILMC 709*) and CD (*FILMCD 709*) reissues under the name *Earthshock* came out from Silva Screen in 1992 with Delia's 'Blue Veils and Golden Sands' and 'The Delian Mode', plus 'The World of *Doctor Who*' (b-side to the *Moonbase 3* theme) as bonus tracks but seems to be harder to find than the vinyl which can be bought for sensible money in good condition.

BBC RADIOPHONIC WORKSHOP – THE SOUND HOUSE: MUSIC FROM THE BBC RADIOPHONIC WORKSHOP
Label: BBC Records
ID: REC467 (LP)/ ZCM 467(cassette)

Roger Limb curated this 1983 compilation that presents one new collaborative piece from the current workshop line-up, and then cherry picks the best of their recent output.

This album destroys the fashionable myth that the synth years saw a drop in quality at the Workshop. Despite being a snapshot of the Workshop in 1983, it packs in an enormous amount of variety. That's because in 1983 commissions were coming in from all sorts of departments. The work here ranges from light entertainment TV programmes to serious radio documentaries via children's television. Science-Fiction was falling out of vogue on television with its only noticeable presence here being two wonderful Paddy Kingsland pieces for *The Hitchhikers Guide to the Galaxy* (which, as a comedy, reached audiences outside the genre).

It is the definite compilation of the synth era of the Radiophonic Workshop, beginning fittingly with 'Radiophonic Rock' where Peter Howell constructs a rhythmic sequence on the Fairlight and then every other composer in the Workshop comes in a does a little turn over the top. It's a cheeky little intro that sets the scene for a fun journey into sound.

A journey that includes everything from Paddy Kingsland's tuba waltz on a synth for the unfortunate Whale in *Hitchhikers* to the beautiful minimalism of Dick Mill's 'Catch The Wind', to Roger Limb's exciting and catchy 'Rallyman' music which makes me want to learn to drive even though I can't and have never otherwise wanted to.

Elizabeth Parker previews her landmark *Planet Earth* soundtrack and also shares her wake up call for the people of Blackburn. A particularly powerful moment is 'The Unseeing Eye', a piece Malcolm Clarke created to accompany the writer Jorge Luis Borges talking about his blindness. A dark, rhythmic piece with strange percussive sounds – 'The Unseeing Eye' could easily be mistaken for some of today's avant-garde music. That this introspective piece is immediately followed by Howell and Mills very beautiful interpretation of 'Fancy Fish' from 'The Carnival Of The Animals' is an inspired change of mood, frankly.

It's not just me who has this album in their DJ bag, either - both Future Sound Of London & Demdike Stare have put 'The Unseeing Eye' in DJ mixes.

Such a shame it's not been reissued....yet. No CD version has ever been produced and while most of it is on the *Retrospective* anthology, the spirit of the album gets lost in the enormous track-listing of *Retrospective* (plus I can never quite make my mind up about the remastering for that CD). If you really want to enjoy the *Sound House* in all its glory, you have either to get the vinyl or the tape.

PADDY KINGSLAND – THE JINGLE MACHINE
Label: KPM Music
ID: KPM1301

Tracklist
A: A collection of jingle melodies
B: Programme cues, station idents and electronic effects

As is clear from the title, this is a library LP of jingles ready made for radio and tv features. Everything about this LP screams 'library use' rather than home listening. For instance, to help producers navigate the LP the track number is spoken before each piece, the titles are specific and deliberate indicators of what kind of music it is, and nearly every track is available in two or three variations.

The first three tracks are all called 'Do It Yourself' for example, and feature brief snappy music arrangements from the sounds of someone doing D.I.Y. 'Visions' offers slightly cheesy cod-mystical sounds, while 'The Blaster' provides tough synth sounds for something more edgy and dark. In passing, only one piece on here passes the minute mark, making this a dizzying whirl.

It makes for a curious experience, especially as you often find yourself listening to slightly different versions of the same song several times in a row, but counteracting that is the fact that it switches from bright, breezy and easy to mean and moody and back again all the time.

There is absolutely some gold on here, tracks that could still be used for today's TV and radio. There are also some tracks that are firmly rooted in the 80s, and would definitely not be acceptable for today's media but is still enjoyable. There is also some stuff here that's not so enjoyable, that would probably only have been suitable for a Wisconsin sport radio station in 1984. I think it's at its best when Kingsland creates tense synth scores for horror and thrillers but the variety is madly fun. Paddy's library music has been used all over the world including Hollywood and it's not hard to see why.

1984

BBC RADIOPHONIC WORKSHOP - THE LIVING PLANET (A PORTRAIT OF EARTH)
Label: BBC Records
ID: REB 496

Tracklist
A1 - The Living Planet (Theme from The Series)
A2 - The Building of The Earth
A3 - The Frozen World
A4 - The Northern Forests
A5 - Jungle
A6 - Seas of Grass
B1 - The Baking Deserts
B2 - The Sky Above
B3 - Sweet Fresh Water
B4 - The Margins of the Land
B5 - Worlds Apart
B6 - The Open Ocean
B7 - New Worlds (Closing Theme from the Series)

Puzzlingly, you usually don't see this album on discographies of the Radiophonic Workshop. Perhaps because its front cover doesn't mention them but the back cover clearly says 'composed and played by Elizabeth Parker, BBC Radiophonic Workshop'. Which is nuts as it is a stunningly beautiful album that would make Vangelis blush with envy. Not to mention, it's a very prestigious job, composing the music for one of the BBC's David Attenborough series. For the benefit of those not from the UK, he has presented many nature documentaries of such quality that he probably has to have reinforced steel shelving to hold all the awards. American viewers probably get his shows with Morgan Freeman or Sigourney Weaver overdubbing him but he is a very big deal for the rest of us and counts Bjork and Barrack

Obama amongst his admirers.

As this was for an epic, twelve part series covering the history of the earth and diversity of vegetation and environments, Elizabeth Parker had to create an enormous amount of work to soundtrack the stunning visuals of volcanoes, cave paintings, deserts, wildebeest migrations, oceans and polar wastelands. It's a major undertaking for one person on their own and this LP represents just a small sample of what she created, barely a track per episode.

As you would imagine, the music is full of awe and wonder, virtually conjuring the images of the TV show in your mind as you listen. Firmly in the style of ambient and new age, it is an album to unwind to. Make sure you get a copy that is at least Very Good Plus condition for the record itself as any scratches would be very frustrating on such fragile but powerful music. It comes in a beautiful gatefold sleeve which folds out to show lots of breathtaking images from the TV series making it a very desirable object so a copy with the sleeve in at least near mint condition is recommended. Sorry, no CD yet.

HI-TECH FX – SOUND EFFECTS NO.29
Label: BBC Records
ID: REC 531

Tracklist
A1 - Computer Bleeps
A2 - Disk Drives

A3 - Drive Activity
A4 - Printers
A5 - Video Games
A6 - Stings
A7 - Heavier Stings
A8 - Whooshes and Zings
A9 - Computer Background FX
B1 - Singularly Simon
B2 - Computer Rant
B3 - Computer Waltz
B4 - Invaders Rock
B5 - Arcadea
B6 - JDC Background
B7 - Fanfares
B8 - Purple Space And White Coronas
B9 - Ascending Asteroids
B10 - Pulsar Patterns
B11 - Through the Black Hole
B12 - Force of the Universe
B13 - "43"

It is strange how meanings change over time, as this 1984 LP demonstrates. The opening section of this album was created so that amateur dramatics producers would have access to the sounds of a cutting edge computer, something most would not be able to afford. Fast forward to the present and the sounds of whirring discs and grinding printers seems wonderfully kitsch and nostalgic, like tram sound effects 10"s were for the previous generation. After this brief section, we get some fake computer game sounds. They sound exactly like someone playing an arcade game of the 1980s, complete with the sound of button pressing, but not any actual real games, for obvious copyright reasons. They are so convincing that for someone such as myself who was a bright eyed little tyke in the golden age of arcade gaming it's like a false memory syndrome committed to vinyl. There is even the sound of a game loading from tape. I am not much of a one for nostalgia but the old days of gaming and computers are too powerful for me and I cannot help but enjoy this side with a warm fuzzy glow of remembrance which is ironic given the concept and title but the future is here so what can you do? This segues into some very electronic sounds.

A series of simple, spacey effects from *Captain Zep* and other shows, mainly simple bleeps and bloops. The curious thing is nobody is credited with the work on side one.

Over on the flip we find two Simon Hancock compositions, starting with 'Singularly Simon' which has an acid house riff and weird wonky bass and electronic brass melodies. His second piece 'Computer Rant' is a very Kraftwerk inspired instrumental with a techy beat. The rest of side two comes from Dick Mills aside from a wildly jolly and exuberant track from Malcolm Clarke with lots of big noises that sound like fruit machines jamming with a seaside organ in the British holiday resort of the future.

These are more experimental pieces of electronic music than sound effects, to be pedantic, but you probably were not interested in this record for your amateur dramatics society adaptation of Dan Dare anyway. What is particularly interesting is that most of the second side is taken up with Dick Mills' compositions. They feel as though Mills has created sound effects and then arranged them into musical pieces, often quite adventurous and abstract ones. Given the amount of time he spent just creating sound effects, you can't blame him for wanting to cut loose a bit and just like his contributions to the compilation albums, he could create cutting edge electronic music just as good as the rest of them when he got a chance.

This release is relatively obscure and rarely turns up in Radiophonic Workshop discographies but anyone who lived through the pioneering days of home computers will find side A oddly compelling and lovers of electronic music can enjoy some prime Dick Mills on side B. It sells comparatively cheaply and was reissued in 1991 by the BBC on CD with the *Tomorrow's World* theme added and renamed *Essential Hi Tech Sound Effects*.

PETER HOWELL – LEGEND
Label: New World Company
ID: NWCD 148
Tracklist
1 – Golden Space
2 – Silver Journeys

The recent success of archival new age compilation *I Am The Center*[97] has done a lot to change record collectors' attitudes towards new age music. As a compilation of the best of the genre, it introduced listeners to a world of tactile music, rich in mood and atmosphere, created with innovative recording techniques. It also prompted a series of album reissues and lead to a dramatic increase in the prices charged for originals. It's due to *I am the Center* that, not long after hearing that album for the first time and learning that Peter Howell had done a new age album (on cassette only), I tracked it down immediately.

The blurb on the cover promised 'an unexcelled musical mirage, an entrancing focus of exquisite sounds'. How could I go wrong? Howell made many lovely psychedelic folk records and so many classic Radiophonic Workshop pieces, after all, some around the same time as this. My expectations were high for something beautiful and blissful.

What I got was the same slightly naff tune played over and over on keyboards set to pan pipes effect. I kept giving the tape another go every few months to see if perhaps my mood had been off and hoping it might win me over but every time I found it a struggle to get through, with the horrible keyboard sound grating more and more as the tape spooled on. It is not peaceful, it is not comforting or stimulating. It is not big or clever. It's best avoided. I hate being rude about the work of an artist that I respect so much but I have to be honest – it really is awful.

I do not hate new age music. I hate muzak. And this is vile, 1980s dentist's waiting room muzak (for all that the cover helpfully has 'new age music' stamped in one corner and 'inspiring radiant pure' in the other. Ignore them – both claims are bare-faced lies.)

PADDY KINGSLAND – STORYTELLERS
Label: KPM Music
ID: KPM 1312

Subtitled 'Imaginative themes depicting the lyrical, dramatic and humorous aspects of fantasy', this LP (created for the KPM library) shows a strong John Williams influence to begin with on side one. There are lots of epic and dramatic strings and, damn it, I wish I could work out where I know them from but all those pieces feel very familiar from somewhere in my childhood. Everyone I play this to who is my age reacts the same way. Kingsland clearly had his finger right on the pulse of what people wanted for soundtracks back then, and It probably got used all over the place.

On side two the strings are swapped for synths and drum machines, a brass band, tuba and such like all conjuring festive joy. Suddenly it's military brass marches and then it ends with an African piece and some Eastern tabla music. It has no radiophonic qualities at all but it sounds like my childhood so I love it but I keep it with my library music collection not my Radiophonic collection (yes, I organise my record collection by genre). It is still wonderful, though, and can easily be picked up at a bargain price.

1986

BBC RADIOPHONIC WORKSHOP - DOCTOR WHO THE MUSIC II
Label: BBC Records
ID: REH 552

Tracklist
A1 - Peter Howell - The Five Doctors
A2 - Jonathan Gibbs/Tim Barry/Jakob Lindberg - The King's Demons
A3 - Malcolm Clarke - Enlightenment
B01 - Jonathan Gibbs - Warriors of the Deep
B02 - Peter Howell - The Awakening
B03 - Malcolm Clarke - Resurrection of The Daleks
B04 - Peter Howell - Planet of Fire
B05 - Roger Limb - Caves of Androzani

My eyes! My eyes! There is no record sleeve more horrible among the Radiophonic Workshop discography than this foul beast. You can even tell what year it is by the primitive digitisation of the Doctors' photos.

Thankfully the music is far less primitive. Things kick off with an extended suite of Peter Howell's music from 'The Five Doctors'. While it might not be every single cue from the special, it feels like a pretty complete soundtrack: you get the strange horn of the Death Zone, the march of the Cybermen, the sound of the time scoop sucking up victims and some nice weird bits that I can't quite place despite having watched the special more times than I can remember, including recently. Jonathan Gibb's hybrid early music meets synth score for 'The King's Demons' sounds great on vinyl, capturing all the details vividly and seeming so much more alive than with everyone talking over it. Side one ends with Malcom Clarke's demented sea shanties and cabin waltzes from 'Enlightenment'. A typically wild ride that met the story so well and sounds even more eccentric when stripped of its dramatic context. Delighted to say this score gets a big wide slice of vinyl so we can enjoy all its lovely mad moments.

Jonathan Gibb's soundtrack for 'Warriors of the Deep' was far and away the best thing about that particular serial, so it's nice to be able to enjoy it stripped of all the visual nonsense that previously accompanied it. It's really tense synth work that encourages nail chewing, so it's a shame that there's only a brief glimpse of the full score, before the tracklist moves onto similar brief sets from other Season 21 stories – at which moment an obsession with military drum sounds really does become a noticeable thing throughout that season's soundtracks.

Not to put too fine a point on it, the scores all begin to blur into one. 'The Awakening', 'Resurrection of the Daleks', 'Planet Of Fire' and 'Caves of Androzani' all strut past with similarly sharp synths and militaristic drum rolls. Which means that, when somebody breaks loose and interjects a brief moment of the abstract or minimalist, such as Malcolm Clarke's build-ups to the Daleks' arrival or Peter Howell's mysterious mood pieces for the landscapes of Sarn, it comes as sweet, sweet relief. This general uniformity contrasts particularly oddly with side one's varied buffet of sounds. Of course, that's not to suggest that any of it is bad, as such, merely that there's less variety on display than might be hoped. In the end, it probably says more about the demands of the *Doctor Who* production office than about our dear Workshop (but side one is definitely the best!).

1989

WHITE NOISE – WHITE NOISE IV: INFERNO
Label: AMP Records
ID: AMP CD-010

Tracklist
1 - Inferno
2 - Off the Wall
3 - Light Mover
4 - The Source
5 - Runes
6 - Opium
7 - Scurry
8 - Charged Particles
9 - Clouds in White Chiffon
10 - Polka Dots
11 - Laughing Gas
12 - Lemmings
13 - Dreamtime

14 - Getting Light
15 - Labyrinth
16 - Gyroscope
17 - Under the Lens
18 - Sanctus
19 - Go for Your Dongle
20 - Shadowlands
21 - Bringer of Darkness

After the previous album's slightly weak opening, Vorhaus pulls out all the stops for a loud, psychedelic and hammering explosion of a first track that is not even a minute long. That done, we suddenly ourselves faced by 'Off The Wall', which sounds like nothing else so much as Moebius & Plank covering Prince! It's weird and funky and it really bloody works! And the next track, 'Light Mover', is like a psychedelic Phillip Glass!

Vorhaus is still on his Fairlight synthesiser but its 1989 and he's been using it since it came out, so manages to take it places nobody else could. The album, as a result, has a mad energy that feels almost punk, although not without occasional mellow moments such as the sublime 'Clouds in White Chiffon'. Vorhaus' humorous side even gets a moment in the sun on 'Laughing Gas' with its oddly treated laughter lost in a fog of sound. That this track is immediately followed by the frankly disturbing 'Lemmings', which needs to be heard on good headphones for maximum claustrophobia and delirium as the sounds reverberate around your head and suddenly explode into heavy stabs that Bernard Hermann would be proud of.

Inferno is a startling album that always seem to have something that you wouldn't expect hidden up its sleeve. As capable of being alarming as relaxing, it was also a minor farewell from Vorhaus, who did not release another album for eleven years afterwards. It has only been released this once and on CD only, so although you are unlikely to find it cheap or even at a normal price these days, it doesn't retail for silly money quite yet, so it shouldn't hurt too much to pick one up.

1993

BBC RADIOPHONIC WORKSHOP – DOCTOR WHO: 30 YEARS AT THE RADIOPHONIC WORKSHOP
Label: BBC Records
ID: BBC CD 871

Strange to think that this CD is now over twenty years old but that does at least go some way to explaining the high price second hand copies garner online (the BBC are seemingly unaware of the concept of second pressings for CDs).

But never mind that for now. The album starts off, as you would expect, with the Delia Derbyshire theme tune and then concerns itself with the Radiophonic Workshop's sound effects from the show's entire run.

As the playlist is once again chronological, it's easy for the dedicated *Doctor Who* fan to work out who or what they are listening to. It's worth noting, however, that as this disc covers the entire original run of *Doctor Who* it does mean that there is a tiny bit of overlap with the extensive first volume of the more widely available *Doctor Who At The Radiophonic Workshop Volume 1* from 2000. In its defence, though, this compilation came first, so you know that the exclusives on here cannot possibly be leftovers – actually there's a plethora of quite startling and wonderful work on here, creating a quick but wide-ranging run through the Workshop's 1960's output, with some fine highlights of Brian Hodgson's excellent effects and moods.

Strangely, though, there is only one piece from the Jon Pertwee era (1970-1974), an extended sound suite from Brian Hodgson. Which is a great shame, as precious little from that time has been officially released.

Dick Mills takes over with the Tom Baker era, and provides such memorable gems as a horrific squelching for 'The Sontaran Experiment' and some trippy bug sounds for 'The Ark In Space'.

Elsewhere, the disc moves through the years until it reaches the final serials with Sylvester McCoy, and even has Peter Howell's haunting music for the 1993 Jon Pertwee radio play 'The Paradise of Death'.

The only place *30 Years* shows its age is in the digital remastering which, while not exactly *bad*, is not as good as the later CDs, and may prove a disappointment to the committed audiophile.

The cd is long out of print and at times sells for quite extraordinary prices. Incidentally, there are two different covers, one featuring Daphne Oram (which is intriguing as this came out almost fifteen years before the first collection of her music, and contains nothing of hers as she left the Workshop long before *Doctor Who* existed) while the other has an awkwardly leering leggy photo of Delia Derbyshire (the latter tends to go for more money). It's a pain to get hold of and all presented in a rather drab package but it is, unfortunately, a bit on the essential side.

CAVENDISH MUSIC LIBRARY - TIME AND SPACE, AFRICA, POISONED PLANET, ETHNIC IMPRESSIONS AND UNDERSEA WORLD

In 1994, with the Radiophonic Workshop struggling to survive as a commercial entity, they produced five themed CDs for the Cavendish Music Library. Each CD's theme made it easy for film production companies to know what the music was suitable for. The five titles were

- 'Time And Space'
- 'Africa'
- 'Poisoned Planet'
- 'Ethnic Impressions'
- 'Undersea World'.

I'm reviewing them as one entity but with a longer than usual review because they were released simultaneously and share the same origins.

Another reason for me to tackle them all at once is because they share many of the same virtues and the problems.

First, let's start with the very important point that these discs were not created with the album listener in mind. They were created as CDs that a film or TV producer could skip through to find the piece they want to illustrate whatever was showing on screen. Each CD therefore contains very similar work and even on occasion variations of the same track. Consequently, the individual discs do make a monotonous listen when absorbed all in one go.

In passing, the CD era was not a golden age for library music – at least for the electronica fan. Gone were the briefer thirty minute LPs, to be replaced by seventy minute CDs. That extra time makes the listening experience a lot less rewarding but bear in mind that they were not made for you or me. That said, there's some very striking work to be unearthed in the midst of this lack of variation.

Really, though, what makes these compilations particularly of interest is their age. The last Radiophonic Workshop release at that point was from 1985 featuring work from the 1984 series of *Doctor Who*. This disc then is the only released work from their final years, and while this may still be from over twenty years ago, those twenty years have seen far fewer major changes in music technology than those of the preceding ten years. In other words, unlike previous releases, they are using pretty similar equipment to electronic musicians these days.

What is noticeable about this work is how far it has strayed from the Workshop's experimental beginnings. In over five hours of music there are barely any traces of discordance or abstraction, apart from on the 'Poisoned Planet' album. Probably the closest contemporary sounds of the era would be from the CD-ROM based computer games coming out of the larger game publishing studios (and anyone who knows anything about the history of gaming will know this is not in any way a derogatory or dismissive comparison!).

So, who are we listening to?

The artists on these CDs are Malcolm Clarke, Peter Howell, Roger Limb, Elizabeth Parker and Richard Attree. As you can imagine, the collection 'Time and Space' is the most appropriately Radiophonic collection, with Malcolm Clarke contributing far more than anyone else. Forget the *Doctor Who* hints of the title, though; this is almost completely different to anything you've heard on that show, apart from a reprise of the majestic dinner party music from the serial 'Enlightenment'. Instead, it's very much modern electronic music with a futurist bent. Here, in fact, Clarke is at times making music remarkably close to a beatless Boards of Canada!

'Undersea World' is a whole CDs worth of oceanic wildlife documentary soundtracks. In fact, given Elizabeth Parker compositions make up the lion's share of this, it could well contain some further work from her epic 'The Living Planet' soundtrack. There was, after all, a whole 55 minute episode for fresh water life and another 55 for the open oceans. Malcolm Clarke contributes a few numbers too, although it is puzzling to see the waltz from 'Enlightenment' turn up again in another arrangement entitled 'Dance of the Sea Horse'

'Poisoned Planet' is a very bleak collection for use in montages of destruction, devastation, death and war. It is also the most experimental of all the albums put out by Cavendish. Malcolm Clarke does a track called 'Flatulence' which sounds like a traumatised survivor playing a trombone in the wreckage of his former world while the ghosts of a million dead flitter around him. Elsewhere, Elizabeth Parker gets incredibly dark with tracks such as 'All Strung Up' (like something from a Colin Potter-produced Nurse with Wound album). She is definitely the dominating presence on here, with a series of disturbing pieces that you can barely credit are from the composer of *The Living Planet*

As you can imagine, the 'Ethnic Impressions' collection is probably the most flawed. If you want flamenco music, do you want it played by a master flamenco guitar player or on a computer? The best moments are those where the composers play fast and loose with their brief and take a more creative, roundabout interpretation of the given genre. Generally speaking, it's the second half of the CD that contains the most interesting tracks. Richard Attree's electronic didgeridoo sound with a sharp beat is great, while Roger Limb creates hypnotic but unnervingly mechanical music credited as being Tibetan but sounding more like a robot meditations on Jupiter's moons - which works for me.

Other highlights include Richard Attree's piece, billed as being for a Japanese water garden, but actually an engaging slice of funky electro. Elizabeth Parker embraces the widescreen with 'Grecian 2001', a stunning piece that mixes Greek arrangements with a sweeping sense of drama. On the more curious side, Malcolm Clarke's 'Cornish Sea Shanty' is actually the waltz from 'Enlightenment' again but this time played using an accordion sound!

Towards the end there are some pieces billed as nightclub music but prepare yourself more for *Miami Vice* than anything from the contemporary dance scene, especially the piece billed as being San Diego 'techno'. Most baffling of all are a couple of hunks of sleazy electro titled 'Stringfellows' and 'On the Front Line'. I hope these titles can be blamed on Cavendish and not on the Workshop!

After that awkwardness, it makes it slightly odd that the 'Africa' album is so solid. On paper it sounds terrible, a BBC workshop of English electronic musicians paying homage to African music. There's something almost puzzling in the fact it turned out so well.

I think the secret is it takes a cinematic and impressionistic approach to its subject rather than glibly digitising African musical traditions. Yes, it doesn't cast any new light on Africa or challenge any stereotypes, but as it was probably intended to be used as a soundtrack to documentaries about the continent, its purpose was never to shake things up but to match a set of preconceived visuals.

The majority of the music comes from Peter Howell, who was involved with a BBC TV Series called *The Africans* which may or may not be where some of this work comes from. To me, it seems closer to Can's approach with their playful Ethnological Forgery series rather than the squirm inducing appropriations of 80s pop stars.

We will never know what the Workshop would have sounded like if it were still active today but this large collection from just a few years before its demise gives the best clue. In its present form it is hard work but a carefully curated playlist from the five albums creates a far more enjoyable experience.

Although the original CDs are hard to come by, the albums have at some point silently slipped into widespread digital distribution and seem to be available from all download outlets in the UK, including the smart phone operating system providers. Search by the album names rather than 'Radiophonic Workshop' as they are credited to Various Artists with Cavendish mentioned in small print as being the record label. You may even have to search by the composers' names to find them. While these are not flawless albums that you will listen to back to back or even all the way through, they are still a part of the Radiophonic Workshop's history and tell the story of the last chapter in their music.

1997

MUSIC FROM THE TOMB OF THE CYBERMEN
Label: Via Satellite
ID : V-Sat ASTRA 3967

Tracklist
Dr. Who Theme
Tardis Interior
Tardis Landing
Tardis Doors Opening
Space Adventure (Parts 1-5)
Palpitations
Astronautics Theme (Parts 1-7)
Desert Storm
Space Time Music (Parts 1-4)
Tardis Take Off
Dr. Who Theme (A New Beginning)

This one doesn't crop up on most Radiophonic Workshop discographies, as it's more famed for featuring the excellent library music that was picked to accompany this serial. However, of the eleven tracks featured on this CD, six of them are Radiophonic Workshop constructions. There are two different versions of Delia's theme arrangement, Dick Mill's TARDIS door opening sound and then Brian Hodgson's TARDIS take-off and landing sound effects. Interestingly, there is also a 'TARDIS interior' sound by Hodgson which does not appear on any of the official Radiophonic Workshop compilations

But, to be fair, the real gems *are* the library music. M.Slavin's 'Space Adventure', for instance, became almost an unofficial Cybermen anthem in the 60s, cropping up in all their early adventures. Its ominous big bass drum and strange unearthly jazz warbles are extremely distinctive and once heard, never forgotten. Though 'Palpatations' by

John Scott is a brief tense moment, there are also some odd, if quite jazzy, hamming lead tunes from E.Sendel and Heinrich Feischner. Wilfred Josephs' 'Space Time Music' is a big orchestral piece which has much more of an epic Hollywood feel than old fashioned British *Doctor Who*, though it is lovely on any level. As you can tell, this is much more of a library music album than a Radiophonic Workshop one but such a good one that it really does not matter if you like *Doctor Who* or not; if you like electronica, you'll enjoy this.

2000

BBC RADIOPHONIC WORKSHOP - DOCTOR WHO AT THE BBC RADIOPHONIC WORKSHOP VOLUME 1: THE EARLY YEARS 1963-1969
Label: The Grey Area
ID : DRWRW 1

A more apt title for this CD would be *Brian Hodgson at the BBC Radiophonic Workshop*. For, while it does feature a few variants of Delia Derbyshire's iconic *Doctor Who* theme and two hauntingly moody pieces of music John Baker made for an episode of Sci-Fi anthology *Out of the Unknown* which got re-appropriated by *Doctor Who* a few years later, everything else is Hodgson. There are two tracks credited as collaborations with Dick Mills and some work composed by Dudley Simpson then realised by

Hodgson but the rest is just Brian, Brian, Brian – and why not?

Would *Doctor Who* have worked without Brian Hodgson? This CD rather suggests it wouldn't. He blended a deeply intuitive understanding of drama with a creative approach to sound design. Science Fiction is a genre that relies on a great deal of persuasion, not least in persuading the viewer to put aside their reservations and accept the impossible stories that followed. A lot of talented cast and crew played their parts in that persuasion but it helps a great deal that Brian Hodgson could craft a sound that somehow perfectly convinces as that of an alien machine working its way through time and space.

This full length CD is almost entirely comprised of sound effects. Attentive readers may recall my criticism of the older sound effects LPs as being more production utilities than enjoyable home listening experiences, but I am glad to say this doesn't apply to this album. This release has been compiled especially as an actual album, not a tool for amateur dramatics. There are no lengthy sections of laser gun sound effects or rocket take offs here. Another reason it works so well, though, is because Hodgson's work for *Doctor Who* blurred the lines between soundtrack and sound effects. A pedantic approach is to say sound effects are diegetic and intended to be sounds occurring in the reality of the drama whilst the soundtrack is heard only by the viewer and is to aid their enjoyment. However, Brian Hodgson's *Doctor Who* work often blurred the lines between the two. There are a lot of pieces on here that are meant to represent field recordings of alien environments but can double up as brief experimental ambient pieces. When he starts doing actual soundtrack work for the story 'The Wheel in Space', for instance, there is no noticeable difference in style to those extraterrestrial atmosphere pieces.

Of course, some of the tracks *are* pure sound effects, but from the melodic mumblings of the Chumblie robots to the strange sound of a Lovecraftian entity enveloping the TARDIS in webbing in the void of space, it's certainly never dull and persistently intriguingly and unusual. Everything is here in the now familiar chronological order which works perfectly for the obsessive *Doctor Who* type's sense of order, but also leads to a varied compilation that goes through distinctive phases. Just about everything on here is an exclusive and its essential not just for *Doctor Who* fans but for Radiophonic Workshop fans too.

Unfortunately, it is currently out of print both from the BBC and from Mute Records who reissued the album after it first went out of print. However, with a bit of patience, you should be able to buy the Mute edition for a reasonably fair price although you are unlikely ever to snap up a bargain. Still, it should be in any fan's collection, so vital is it in presenting one important era in the history of the Workshop.

BBC RADIOPHONIC WORKSHOP - DOCTOR WHO AT THE RADIOPHONIC WORKSHOP VOL.2 - NEW BEGINNINGS 1970-1980
Label: The Grey Area
ID : DRWRW 2

Part two - the Seventies.

The CD kicks off with the slightly different version of Derbyshire's theme tune, the one with a slight stutter effect at the start. From there, we're straight into Jon Pertwee's first series and the apocalyptic story 'Inferno', represented by Brian Hodgson's sound effect for the disembodied TARDIS console smashing its way into an alternative universe. It's a hard effect to describe, which, I think, proves Hodgson did the job perfectly. The CD also contains Derbyshire's 'Blue Veils and Golden Sands' and 'The Delian Mode' again which were reused for 'Inferno'. Such is the power of these classics that their recurrence here feels welcome. I don't care if own them multiple timest they're worth it. I am sure I will buy them yet again at some point. Why not?

Next serial featured is 'The Mind of Evil', where regular *Who* composer Dudley Simpson realised his score at the Workshop with the help of Dick Mills. It's usually remembered as dark and tense but also has a theme for Dover Castle that is strangely elegant and noisy at the same time.

There is a brief section of Dudley/Dick music for 'The Claws of Axos' and a couple of suitably cosmic sounds from Brian Hodgson and then comes the main feature of the CD - the complete and uncut soundtrack for 'The Sea Devils'. Not only that but it has been discreetly turned into stereo.

It's wild, discordant and at times very noisy. Did the producer have it cut because he was worried people might mistake it for sound effects or because it was so nuts? It's been suggested he was worried it sounded too much like sound effects, but in 2015 that is hard to hear. It's almost awkward how far ahead of its time it is and easily qualifies as the most extreme music created at the Radiophonic Workshop. Its genius certainly won't be appreciated by all but it really is a piece of avant-garde electronic music that deserves the beautiful remastering it gets here. The show would go through two more changes of Production team before the Workshop was asked to create a soundtrack again.

After that we get the justly rejected Delaware version of the *Doctor Who* theme (as featured on the *30 Years* compilation) and some of Dick Mills' special sound work. The CD then focusses on Peter Howell, starting with the demos he made for the *Doctor Who* production office (his alternative soundtrack for 'The Horns of Nimon' is the reason the Workshop were asked to take over from Dudley Simpson and provide the show's soundtracks). Finally, the CD closes with Howell's triumphant new version of the *Doctor Who* theme.

This compilation does repeat a lot from previous releases but the 'Sea Devils' soundtrack in its full splendour is worth the price alone. Which makes everything else by way of a bonus but with true greatness hidden within.

2002

DOCTOR WHO AT THE RADIOPHONIC WORKSHOP VOL.3: THE LEISURE HIVE

Label: BBC Music
ID : WMSF 6052-2

A sudden change of time scale from the previous two decade stretching compilations, this one is entirely focussed on one story. 'The Leisure Hive' is perhaps most significant musically for debuting Peter Howell's remarkable (and brave) version of the classic *Doctor Who* theme but he also composed the incidental music for the serial. Within his first three minute piece for the soundtrack, he has managed to pay a nod to his psychedelic folk roots, riffed on 'Oh I do like to be beside the seaside' and generated cosmic terror. It was the third ever *Doctor Who* serial to get a Radiophonic soundtrack (after 1968's 'The Wheel in Space' and 1972's magisterial 'The Sea Devils') and Howell sounds like he's pulling out all the stops with this rare opportunity.

The utopian society presented in the serial is accompanied by extremely beautiful and euphoric synthesiser music of the first order. As the story gets progressively darker, we get totalitarian stomps, lots of whooshes and dark, rolling moods to match the drama. By their own admission, the Workshop regularly had such tight deadlines for scoring *Doctor Who* that they had to rush the soundtracks but 'The Leisure Hive' feels like it was made with all the time in the world, with a deep attention to detail and a whole host of ideas.

The end credits toll and you instinctively feel like you have reached the end of the CD but you haven't, because next comes Dick Mills and his special sounds., beginning with the howling winds of the planet Argolis, all stark and inhospitable, which are suddenly disturbed by the sound of an earth shuttle arriving with every warning sounds honking away lest some alien life form get squashed flat. It's quite disturbing stuff, especially the distorted heavy breathing and alien pulse of 'Operating Room'.

The remastering is wonderful and a feast for the ears. It's a shame this CD has never been reissued, though, as Mute Records only re-released the first two volumes. As a result, it now languishes in obscurity and is sold for some at times ridiculous second hand prices.

In summary, people need to get over their fear of the Radiophonic Workshop's synth period and this needs to come out again.

BBC RADIOPHONIC WORKSHOP – DOCTOR WHO AT THE RADIOPHONIC WORKSHOP VOL.4: MEGLOS AND FULL CIRCLE
Label: BBC Music
ID : WMSF 6053-2

The final volume of the BBCs Radiophonic Workshop Doctor Who series focuses on two serials: 'Meglos', a wonderful tale of a megalomaniac cactus, and 'Full Circle', a more thoughtful science fiction story. Interestingly, the soundtrack for 'Meglos', whilst mostly created by Peter Howell, also had contributions from Paddy Kingsland. Kingsland's work is the more tense and percussive sounding nd works very effectively in evoking a claustrophobic sense of evil and doom. His pieces are quite spooky with all sorts of unexpected stabs of sound suddenly jumping in.

Peter Howell's work on 'Meglos' meanwhile conjures up the strange and macabre religious rites performed within the serial. Vocoder chants and distorted drums underpin the ominous synth work. Weird, discordant explosions of sound suddenly loom in the speakers, adding to the sensation of menace and fear.

Over on the somewhat less interesting, though still excellent, 'Full Circle', Kingsland conjures up a strange, primordial Eden with his synth sounds, giving a pastoral feel to them when not busy doing marching monster music.

So, what happened? Why did volumes 1 and 2 get reissues and not these? Why no volume 5? Well, the first two volumes were clearly cherry picked from the Workshops popular golden age. Their reach was broad, appealing to *Doctor Who* fans and lovers of experimental music. These third and fourth volumes, however, are perhaps a little too thorough, too completist for a musical era that has yet to find much appreciation beyond the realm of fandom.

Whilst volume 3 created more variety by including much of Dick Mills' special sound, this fourth volume is in the end a bit too.....samey. There are plenty of great moments but to sit and listen to the entire CD all the way through is an underwhelming experience.

The prices it goes for these days are out of all proportion to the pleasure it can provide. This is purely down to *Doctor Who* fans and their compulsive completist urges. It has never been reissued and it goes for insane prices.

2003

BBC RADIOPHONIC WORKSHOP - MUSIC FROM THE RADIOPHONIC WORKSHOP
Label: Rephlex
ID: CAT 147 LP

This box set release on Aphex Twin's Rephlex record label consists of two existing compilations, 1969's 'pink' album and 1975's *The Radiophonic Workshop*.

However, what is interesting about it is that it splits them across a collection of four ten inch records and rearranges the tracklist so that everything is ordered by composer. So, Delia Derbyshire takes up all of side A and side B, John Baker gets side C and D and so on. While the original running orders are perfect for album listening, they don't give you much of a sense of who you are listening to as brief tracks whizz by. This release makes the listener acutely aware of the composer they are hearing, which is an excellent idea.

The other noteworthy thing about it is features all the bonus tracks that were included on the CD reissues, making this their only outing on vinyl. It sold out fairly fast when it came out but there are second hand copies coming up for sale all the time, usually at pretty reasonable prices too.

TRISTRAM CARY – DOCTOR WHO: DEVILS' PLANETS - THE MUSIC OF TRISTRAM CARY
Label: BBC Music
ID: WMSF 6072-2

Although not usually listed as part of the BBC Radiophonic Workshop's discography, it features Delia Derbyshire's familiar opening and closing credits plus three Brian Hodgson sound effects created for 1963's 'The Daleks'.

This is, in fact, far more Radiophonic Workshop content than the *Doctor Who 25th Anniversary* album which somehow sneaks onto discographies (but not this one)!

While never a member of the Workshop or even a collaborator (except while discussing their respective work on 'The Daleks' with Brian Hodgson), Cary was a founder of EMS who provided classic synths to the Workshop and his work is guaranteed to appeal to anyone who enjoys the Workshop's early output.

In fact, Cary's score for 'The Daleks' is so abstract, experimental and electronic that it is commonly mistaken by viewers as being the handiwork of the Radiophonic Workshop. While Brian Hodgson created the Dalek voices and the evil hum on the Dalek's control room and corridors, not to mention the eerie howling of winds for the dead forest (all includes on here), Cary created the celestial abstractions you hear when the Dalek city is viewed from a distance. His score for The Daleks' is compulsively brilliant, full of strange twists and sounds.

Along with Brian Hodgson's work it provides a timeless sonic backing for the story (which founders when stripped of them for the film remake with Peter Cushing).

Although created a mere two years later, his score for 'The Daleks Masterplan' is wildly different. Here he has the use of horns, strings, piano and percussion as well as electronics and varies his approach to fit the wildly differing locations provided by the epic twelve episode story.

Indeed, Cary provides everything from dark space atmosphere to a silent comedy film romp via ancient Egypt and industrial Manchester. The electronics are tense at times, almost industrial, especially the climax. It's a huge shame that nearly all the TV episodes are missing from the archives because the addition of visuals really would have hammered home to *Doctor Who* fans what a talented composer Cary was.

His third and final score for *Doctor Who* was a full seven years later, for Jon Pertwee story 'The Mutants' in 1972. This one is a suitably mental all electronic odyssey which compliments the lo-fi psychedelic feel of the serial. It's really quite wigged out in places with chattering synth drones creating a trippy atmosphere, contrasting with some dark drones for the more dramatic scenes.

It's a great double CD album but unfortunately, there is a catch. It's been out of print for a few years now and as it appeals to two different types of obsessive collectors, *Doctor Who* fans and experimental music fans.

As a result, it tends to show up only at shocking asking prices. That's a real shame, as Cary's contributions to both *Doctor Who* and electronic music are widely overlooked.

2004

FRIENDS – FRAGILE
Label: ACME
ID: ACLN1007CD

Tracklist
1 - You Need Friends
2 - A Tale of Your Life
3 - Summer Sunday Blues
4 - One Sweet Day
5 - Memories
6 - Lonely Road
7 - In the Morning
8 - Come Inside
9 - Take a Walk

10 - River Song
11 - Once in a Winter Town
12 - Time to Run

The final album to emerge from the collaboration between Peter Howell and John Ferdinando. Although dating from 1972, this album was abandoned when Howell joined the Radiophonic Workshop and did not see the light of day until 2004, well over ten years after the first reissues of Agincourt and Ithaca. The big surprise is that what we have here is a fully-formed, completed album ready to be enjoyed in all its splendour. Not only that, but it is arguably the finest pre-Workshop album Peter Howell was involved in.

It is a surprising album with some quite rocky numbers such as 'Lonely Road' with its hard drums, fast acoustic guitar and fuzzy guitar sounds. 'Memories' has a percussive section to match 'Sympathy For the Devil' and an irresistible singalong set of verses over a deep, low funky bass. With this in mind, it's interesting that John Ferdinando received no writing credits on *Fragile*, with all songs written by Howell except for two he co-wrote with singer Ruth Cubbin. *Doctor Who* fans will be intrigued to hear there is a song on here called 'River Song' - a wistful ballad and surely some coincidence?

The digital transfer for the CD version is really lovely, capturing lots of detail and atmosphere. The most tantalising thing about *Fragile* is that it begs the question – if Howell had not joined the Radiophonic Workshop, did a career in mainstream music beckon?

2007

DAPHNE ORAM – ORAMICS
Label: Paradigm Discs
ID: PD21

This double CD compilation was the world's first taste of the Daphne Oram archive.

Before 2007, she was just an obscure inventor, theorist and minor footnote in the official history of the Radiophonic Workshop, but this single release changed all of that. Working through an enormous archive, Clive at Paradigm Discs carefully selected an exciting and diverse body of work to fill up two CDs with enormously impressive and enjoyable experimental music. Derived from both her personal experiments, her commercial commissions and her work with schools, Paradigm present everything from minimalist abstraction and terrifying, treated percussive works right up to the special sound for a 1966 Lego commercial and Daphne doing live manipulation of audience members voices up on stage. The material here shows she was capable of being playful and melodic, subtle and rhythmic but could also easily break with all tradition and form and absolutely let rip. Frankly, there is material on here that could be classified as noise.

Right from the word go, this compilation beguiles and bewilders. Its gentle opening, for example, is followed by a brief melodic track accompanied by power tools.

Then you get the epic thirteen minute 'Birds of Parallax', which was used for the ballet 'Xallaraparallax' and takes in all kinds of strange sounds, from melodic beat tracks to abstract spaced periods. 'Contrasts Essconic' showcases the harsher end of her music with loud, echoing sounds like a robot attacking a piano with tape manipulation assaults suddenly crashing in and then vanishing. This compilation playfully follows it up with her sound for a 1966 Lego commercial and then more strange ballet soundtracks.

Daphne Oram's work is not for the faint-hearted, as it can be very piercing and also overwhelmingly intense at times. Her 'Four Aspects' piece is particularly claustrophobic as it builds and builds into an abstract cacophony of low end sound. There's some strange chattering, giggling voices for a production of *Doctor Faustus* that no-one should listen to if they're suffering from sleep-deprivation. Yet there are also moments of beauty, melody and perfect electronic rhythms. Perhaps the most playful thing on here is her soundtrack for the short film *Snow* which sees her time stretch a piece of music loosely based on rock 'n' roll instrumental 'Teen Beat' by Sandy Nelson, increasing the pace to fit the visuals, moving from sluggish all the way up to frenetic towards the end.

The remastering is terrific and with plenty of sleeve notes, the CD version is a pretty comprehensive release. It's now out of print but not too hard to track down at a normal price, although it's not something you are every likely to find in a bargain bin. Young Americans issued a vinyl version of this album as a four disc set which I don't own but am told lacks the sleeve notes of the CD version. Whatever format you have it on doesn't really matter. What does matter is that you have this reputation-defining compilation in your music collection

LILY GREENHAM - LINGUAL MUSIC
Label: Paradigm Music
ID : PD 22

Currently the most extreme release relating to the Radiophonic Workshop, the archives of Lily Greenham were kept alongside Daphne Oram's by the late Hugh Davis and this compilation came out alongside the first Daphne anthology on Paradigm Discs.
 Greenham's work is difficult to describe without hearing it, though the term 'sound poetry' is often used. This is a strange kind of poetry though where the rhythm and delivery of the words is more important than the words themselves. It's certainly a very divisive form of avant-garde spoken word which only those with a taste for the extreme side of art should seek out. The Workshop connection comes via seven tracks which feature electronics by Paddy Kingsland (as they date back to the 70s they may even have been Workshop productions).
 There is also a 1974 piece made with Richard Yeoman Clark which is definitely a BBC Radiophonic Workshop piece and won an honorary award at the

international contest for electro-acoustic music in Bourges in 1975.

Some tracks are simply Greenham rolling words around on her tongue strangely, while others involve intense electronic manipulation of sound to blast the listener with a rapid fire delivery of distorted words. If you are the sort of person who has been using the Nurse With Wound list as your shopping directive then you'll feel perfectly at home in Lily Greenham's mad world. If on the other hand, you are hoping for anything that resembles any of the Workshop's other commercially released work then you will be in for a major shock. However, it has to be said that her piece with Yeoman-Clark's assistance, 'Relativity', really is a startling highlight, the multi-tracked voices layered around like textures. It's mad and arty but if you can take that sort of thing it's also damn good.

2008

BBC RADIOPHONIC WORKSHOP – A RETROSPECTIVE
Label: The Grey Area
ID: Phonic3cd

Following on from the cherished *Doctor Who at the Radiophonic Workshop* series comes this awkward, ugly little sibling from 2008. Let's be charitable and start with the good points, though. There is a wealth of previously unreleased and incredibly rare material on here. Daphne Oram finally gets a look in on a Radiophonic Workshop compilation, rightfully opening it with her piece for TV show *Amphitryon 38*. She may have created it before the Radiophonic Workshop actually existed, but it still feels like overdue and richly deserved recognition (intriguingly, the next track 'The Ocean' is credited to both Oram and Desmond Briscoe).

It's also a nice touch that the compilation contains plenty of unreleased material from the later years, with Elizabeth Parker and Richard Attree featured heavily. An extended suite of music from cult classic *The Changes* is gratefully received and it's nice to have a Delia Derbyshire rarity, 'Dance From Noah', although it's not strictly a Radiophonic Workshop track and was made for a demonstration LP to showcase the VCS3.

All that said, however, 'A Retrospective' is not short of problems. Most glaringly, a large chunk of the tracklist is taken up by the inclusion of almost all of the *21* and *Soundhouse* compilations. Now don't get me wrong, they are great compilations and the material deserves hearing by a wider audience, so their inclusion here does grant them more exposure but it also creates a definite conflict for the more dedicated fan. If you own *A Retrospective* then you own all but a couple of tracks from those compilations but the absences themselves are odd. *21* only loses the incidental music from 'Mind Of Evil' which is unusual, but you can only fit so much on a CD and I appreciate some difficult decisions have to be made. However, my favourite track from *Soundhouse*

('Rallyman') is missing, and I am not so sure about the remastering of the *Soundhouse* material in general. It's fine for a background listen or on a smaller hi-fi but when paying attention on good hi-fi it can sometimes feel a little lacking.

All the other remastering is fine with some intelligent treatment of the early works and as the later material was recorded in digital formats anyway, there's no issues with it. The compilation becomes particularly interesting for the last twenty or so tracks which were all previously unreleased, giving us a vivid portrait of the final years of the Workshop before Producer Choice snuffed it out. Obviously, being tasked with the mission of creating a two CD set summing up the entire Radiophonic Workshop was an impossible task for anyone so you have to make allowances. Really, what was needed was not a two CD album but a box set.

A very big box set.

JOHN BAKER - THE JOHN BAKER TAPES VOLUME 1: BBC RADIOPHONICS
Label: Trunk Records
ID: JBH028CD

Another heroic presentation from Trunk Records. This CD is jammed to capacity with music from Baker's stint at the Radiophonic Workshop, which lasted from 1963 to 1974. Virtually none of this had ever been commercially released before, but lovingly curated and nicely mastered, it makes a strong case for Baker's talents whilst also being a hell of a lot of fun. There *are* stereotypical electronic space atmosphere sounds but also lots of bright, breezy songs with catchy melodies and quirky arrangements. It's hugely listenable and immensely varied.

Baker's creative knack for witty arrangements from ruler twangs and booze bottles is only one side of his talent. He came from a jazz background and never hesitated to add real instruments to his productions, letting the radiophonics be just one member of the band.

Whether he's doing piano for a song about how to pronounce your vowels for a children's education programme or creating a terrifying, dark theme tune for an adaptation of *Dial M for Murder* which would make John Barry jealous, he always seems in his element. Even more extraordinary than those is 'Scene (Never Never)' which sees his brother on vocals while John backs him with beats and electronics. It's the birth of electro pop and was only heard by sixth formers back in the day.

Although Baker's presence on the original Radiophonic Workshop album was very noticeable, it didn't quite put across his full, extensive range. This forty nine track, seventy two minute beauty goes some way to balancing the books and showing us exactly what he did at the Radiophonic Workshop.

Sadly, this CD is now out of print and even second hand this one usually gets marked up quite a bit, but with patience and diligence you will eventually get it at a normal price. There is also an LP version that takes the best parts part of Volumes one and two which takes similar hunting.

JOHN BAKER - THE JOHN BAKER TAPES VOLUME 2: SOUNDTRACKS, LIBRARY, HOME RECORDINGS, ELECTRO ADS
Label: Trunk Records
ID: JBH029CD

The second volume of the extensive John Baker anthology takes a look at what he did outside the Workshop. The flexible working hours of the Workshop gave Baker the opportunity to do a lot of moonlighting. There's some jazz recordings with the Weinberger Jazz Duo, lots of pounding electronic tracks from his releases for the Southern Library (recorded under the name John Matthews) and – as the sub-title suggests - his advert work.

Obviously, to fully enjoy this compilation, the listener must have an appreciation for jazz. Jazz-a-phobes will struggle with the seven numbers on here but surely even they will be able to appreciate John's virtuosity on the piano. The duo numbers are very mellow, Sunday afternoon sounds and even includes a Beatles medley. On the other side of jazz there is the moody soundtrack he composed for Ridley Scott's short film *Boy On A Bicycle*, with a full jazz band which sounds great.

The library music too is fantastic, and includes some of his very best electronic work. The rhythms seem snappier and sharper than his BBC work, much more along the lines of 90s dance music, in fact. These, and some of the home demos, frequently astonish with their excessive futurism. One unfinished piece from the 60s particularly sounds like something from forty years later.

The compilation brings a poignant close to the Baker saga by finishing with a home recording of John at the piano from the 80s, possibly his last recording. Then we hear his brother Richard Anthony Baker presenting a short obituary for John on his BBC Radio 5 Live show before it all ends with a 1954 recording of a 16 year old Baker.

While volume one is out of print and regularly overpriced by sellers, this volume remains in print and cheap. If you're one of those people who only own Volume 1 then its time you did something about it. It's the second volume but its first rate.

2010

DAPHNE ORAM/BELBURY POLY – SPACESHIP UK: THE UNTOLD STORY OF THE BRITISH SPACE PROGRAMME

Label: Sound and Music
ID: SB01

Tracklist
A1 - Daphne Oram - Look At Life

A2 - Daphne Oram - Manchester I: Single Cymbals Bite Study
A3 - Belbury Poly – Monstroon

A very awkward record to find as it seems to have been made for promotional purposes and distributed only at the Sonar Festival in 2010 to promote British electronic music (the booklet even tells you where and when you can see British electronic acts at the festival that year). Unfortunately, it is a slight but essential item because it features two very, VERY brief excerpts from otherwise unreleased Daphne Oram works. The first extract is 40 seconds long and is quite harsh, almost industrial with its crashing dithyrambic percussion and odd string sounds. The second extract is almost two minutes of hallucinogenic space noises, like bells chiming on an LSD soaked asteroid. It builds and builds until it ends with a dramatic boom that sounds like a treated piano.
The majority of the record (it's single sided and plays at 33rpm) is taken up with a really solid track from Belbury Poly which blends tribal percussion, old radiophonic style abstract space sounds and a ghostly electronic organ pumping out the melodies. It's a prime slice of what is widely known as hauntology music and comes accompanied by an essay that gives the record its name, explaining the history of British electronic music.

This is not a cheap record to get your hands on but it does look nice. Perhaps it might be worth holding off for now and hopefully somebody will release the full pieces featured on here in their entirety for commercial release in the near future.

2011

DAPHNE ORAM – THE ORAM TAPES VOLUME ONE
Label: Young Americans
ID: YoungAm003

Following on from 2007's defining compilation *Oramics*, this new collection was compiled and released by Young Americans (an offshoot of online store Boomkat). People often categorise this one as being focussed on the darker side of her music and while it's not all vintage noise, the majority of it is on the harsher and darker side, so if *Oramics* made you wince a few times you could struggle with this. There are some absolute treats, though, such as 1963's 'New Atlantis' which celebrates that Francis Bacon essay you've heard all about with such elegant sound treatments and sonic soundscapes that it makes the heart soar. There are also some of her disturbing sound effects for classic black and white film *The Innocents*.

When it comes to dark and noisy, *The Oram Tapes Volume One* definitely pushes the envelope. The same innovation and experimentation is demonstrated but the results are surprising to the modern ear. This must have been downright shocking back then too, even to those used to Stockhausen or Xenakis, though this is not quite the vital masterwork that *Oramics* was, simply because that album did such a good job of obtaining the best works. Some tracks on this disc approach redundancy, in fact. An excerpt of 'Electronic Sound Patterns' is provided but the full original is now widely available (and cheap to download). The track 'Pulse Persephone' from *Oramics* reoccurs on both discs here both in its component parts and as a pitched experiment. A recording of a baby being born is presented without much sound treatment. Of course, I'm being picky; this is another much needed anthology from Daphne Oram's archives and full of sterling work. It's also worth mentioning how beautiful and elaborate the CD edition is. Having taken a peek at them myself, I sincerely hope more volumes eventually follow and if I seem overly critical in this review it is just to get you ready to listen to it. It's not *Oramics* but it is gushing with genius.

2013

THE KROTONS
(credited to Brian Hodgson and the BBC Radiophonic Workshop)
Label: Silva Screen
ID: SILCD1371 (cd) / SILLP1371 (10" vinyl)

In 2013 Silva Screen Records made the surprising announcement that they were going to release two albums, each containing an entire soundtrack from a *Doctor Who* serial. Although the BBC had attempted something similar with the *Doctor Who at the Radiophonic Workshop* series, that seemed to quickly fizzle out. Even more unexpected was the choice of *The Krotons* as one of the first releases, presenting all of Brian Hodgson's special sound on one CD or, even better, on a ten inch record. It really is a release that demands we use the term 'special sound' because these are not in any way conventional sound effects. Instead they are short pieces of highly atmospheric *musique concrète*.

Some are strange reverberating waltzes and others are harsh industrial pieces. Peculiar bubbling sounds, deep space pulses and mechanical evil hums away. As the shorter format of the vinyl edition signposts, this is a pretty brief release, a mini-album as they used to say, but brevity is a great enhancer of experimental music. It's still going to be tough going for the casual music fan who likes something with a nice tune and a good beat, but has no sentimental attachment to 1960's *Doctor Who*, but it will be food and drink for those who like their experimental music that little bit darker.

BBC RADIOPHONIC WORKSHOP – THE CAVES OF ANDROZANI
(credited to Roger Limb and the BBC Radiophonic Workshop)
Label: Silva Screen
ID: SILCD1370 (cd) / SILLP1370 (2 x 12" vinyl)

Released in tandem with the *The Krotons* soundtrack, making the two releases quite a yin and yang to each other. The previous release squeezed easily onto one ten inch record and featured unearthly sounds. This epic beast spreads out across two twelve inch records and is packed with dark, moody synths and tense drums. It is an obvious choice for a dedicated soundtrack release, given its evergreen popularity with *Doctor Who* fans, but as it features every single cue of music from the serial, it does start to become quite a hardcore release. Obviously, Roger Limb's soundtrack is a sterling piece of work and the remastering for the CD version is extremely vivid and punchy, while the vinyl version is a little flatter but not bad with a pleasantly old fashioned analogue feel to it.

It is just a question of whether this is a bit of an overdose. You can hop in at any point during this soundtrack and here something very powerful and dramatic but to listen to it all in one go is something that perhaps only those of us who are dedicated *Doctor Who* fans are likely to do. As someone who collects soundtrack LPs from all sorts of era and genres, the recent trend for doing a big 'every single cue' release is not something I particularly love. Death Waltz did it best when they released John Carpenter's soundtrack for *The Fog* with the classic soundtrack selection on the first LP and then the extreme every-other-cue selection on the second LP. That way you can dip in and enjoy the highlights any time and when you're feeling dedicated you can stick on the second LP. This is a classic soundtrack, just laid on a bit thick.

2014

DELIA DERBYSHIRE & ANTHONY NEWLEY - MOOGIES BLOOGIES
Label: Trunk Records
ID: TTT008

Tracklist
A1 - Moogie Bloogies
A2 - I Decoded You (Moogie Bloogies Part 2)

A long famed collaboration between Anthony Newley (the man who co-wrote 'Feeling Good', inspired David Bowie and starred in surreal comedy, *The Strange World of Gurney Slade*) and Delia Derbyshire which has been around on the internet in a slightly scrappy mp3 version for a few years. Newley had a confusing career that straddled comedy and pop music and this sad but lusty song seems to continue blurring the lines. Newley seems melancholically perverted and wistful while Delia creates a beautiful, bass-heavy pop melody for him to play around over. Heart-breakingly, it is only a demo that he made before moving to America with Joan Collins. It seems pretty wonderful and perfect to me so I can't imagine what a 'finished' version might have sounded like. Probably a horrible compromise with too many cooks but Delia was left disappointed and wondering what might have been.

The b-side however, came as complete news to me. Another Newley vocal but this time leaning towards his very surreal sense of humour with Delia following suit and creating a brief waltz which the experts at Trunk think is actually sampling Henk Badings, which throws a new light on 1960's techniques. It goes without saying, the collision of these two immense talents is wonderful and while just recorded as home demos, Delia's idea of a home demo is better than most's idea of studio recording. When this record was announced my heart fluttered and it did not disappoint. Hats off to all involved from inception to release.

DELIA DERBYSHIRE – THE DELIAN MODE
Label: Silva Screen
ID: SIL71458

Very much a modern phenomenon, this 7" takes two previously released classics, 'The Delian Mode' and 'Blue Veils And Golden Sands', and puts them together on a record with wonderful sleeve art and threateningly limited availability. It sold out straight away and spawned a very nice t-shirt but as anyone who likes Delia Derbyshire should have these two songs anyway, this is more a collectable artefact than a means of obtaining music for listening to. There is nothing wrong with that, though; I like the fact that these two holy grails of electronic music are being worshiped in this way.

No, I do not endorse paying the crazy second hand prices for it but I like that this exists and that it is being fetishized in this way because the musical contents are worthy of the upmost respect and reverence.

DELIA DERBYSHIRE & BARRY BERMANGE – THE DREAMS

Label: Psychic Sounds
ID: PSR012

Tracklist
A1 - Running
A2 - Land
A3 - Falling
B1 - Sea
B2 - Colour

The Dreams is the first part of Barry Bermange's 'Inventions for Radio' series created for the BBC's Third Programme. Barry collected a series of interviews with people where they describe their dreams. Delia then takes the interviews and reassembles them over a dark and terrifying musical background.

'The Nightmares' might be a better title for the first part. It deals with dreams of falling, of being chased and I cannot play it in the presence of my four year old because it gives him the heebie-jeebies. The surreal reassembled and repeated descriptions are quite disturbing and a tense, humming heartbeat pulses away inhumanely beneath the accounts. The voices are always interesting, never jarring or irritating – indeed, they are perhaps a little too good. Are these real interviews or actors reading transcripts from real interviews? There is music in their voices or is it the rhythmic alchemy of Delia's editing?

A sudden pause and we are into accounts of falling, accompanied by what sounds like dead souls howling around wreckage of a ruined earth. It is not a comforting listen at any point. The fifth moment is mostly about dreams of drowning set to haunting, echoing tones. A shorter instrumental version of which was released as 'The Delian Mode' for the 'pink' album and reoccurs on other compilations. If anyone were ever able to recreate the soundtrack of your dreams, it was surely Delia Derbyshire. 'The Dreams' is a curious beast, part electronic album and part experimental drama, equally easy to appreciate as both and timelessly haunting.

Not quite sure how official these recent vinyl issues are from a couple of small American record labels. I picked one of them up and it had no copyright information on it at all so either there is no copyright for the material in America or it's a complete bootleg. The version I got (with cover artwork more befitting some psychedelic rock group) had fairly basic sound quality, quite flat and distinctly inferior to the last repeat of the programme on radio.

No CD version has been issued at the time of writing, official or otherwise, sadly.

ROBERTO GERHARD - ELECTRONIC EXPLORATIONS FROM HIS STUDIO + THE BBC RADIOPHONIC WORKSHOP 1958-1967
Label: Sub Rosa
ID: SRV378

Apart from the Workshop staff and composer Tristam Carey, one of the few people in Britain working with electronic music was Spanish composer Roberto Gerhard. Gerhard was a very well respected avant-garde composer and friends with such distinguished Spanish artists as Joan Miró and Pablo Casals. However, as a supporter of the Republicans in the Spanish civil war, he had to flee his home country when Franco came to power. After a brief time in France, he made his home in England.

Here he began to experiment with electronic music and as he was on good terms with the BBC, frequently receiving soundtrack commissions from them and letting his recordings be used as stock music for *Doctor Who*, he became the only outside composer to be given access to the BBC Radiophonic Workshop.

The six tracks compiled here provide a brief but fascinating collection of wild, experimental electronic music. Gerhard's experiments feel far less academic and more alive and vibrant than Stockhausen's rather aloof works. The sounds are just as alien but there is so much passion and emotion here. It's a living experimental music.

The restoration work done at the University of Huddersfield's Centre for Research in New Music is, frankly, astounding. The CD sound gives the pieces a life that belies their age.

Unfortunately, details for much of the music here is lost to time. Gerhard kept little paperwork relating to his music and this material was all taken from his personal tapes. As such it's not possible to give full and clear credits for most of the music which makes its debut here (this is the first time his sound collages have been released). It does come with a decent sized booklet, explaining the history and context of Gerhard's work. In addition, Desmond Briscoe in the 25th anniversary Radiophonic Workshop book does mention them assisting Gerhard with the last (and by far longest) track on here, 'Lament For The Death Of A Bullfighter' and also refers to Dick Mills performing live with a symphony orchestra as part of a new Gerhard work. Sadly, his collaboration with Delia Derbyshire on the soundtrack of the radio play *The Anger of Achilles* is absent but hopefully this means there will be a follow up compilation.

As it was released in October 2014, both the CD and silver vinyl edition are widely available at the time of writing but like most releases in the modern age, they will be limited.

RADIOPHONIC WORKSHOP
Label: N/A
ID: N/A

A bit of a curious one, this. It's not the much alluded to new album which is referred to in all the publicity and interviews for the current live unit that is known simply as the Radiophonic Workshop. Instead, this is an album they created for speaker manufacturers Bowers & Wilkins subscription service (a service made available for free for a few months to people who purchase Bowers & Wilkins products or to paying subscribers). Available only in high quality flac files or Apple lossless, the idea being that the superior quality files would allow people to get full benefit from their Bowers and Wilkins' speakers.

This leaves us to consider whether or not we should consider this a proper album or just a promotional tool used perhaps to help cover the costs of the recording of the 'real' Radiophonic Workshop album we keep hearing about, the one with guest appearances from contemporary artists like Andrew Weatherall, Hot Chip and Ghostpoet. Going by the quality levels on here, I think its best we consider this just a discreet, minor release.

It starts off quite promisingly with 'On' a brief, spooky piece of manipulated voices and dark, unearthly sound. This segues right into 'Out There' which begins with more abstracted electronic sound and gets even harsher as it progresses. It does have that classic, strange, alienated sound of the Radiophonic Workshop taken into modern high-fidelity and it is genuinely great. Then things begin to go very, very wrong.

Suddenly Delia Derbyshire's 'Ziwzih Ziwzih OO-OO-OO' starts playing. Not a cover version, the actual song. It gets about forty of so seconds unaccompanied and then suddenly in come some slow, plodding rock drums and a load of keyboards playing the riff in the most awkwardly, clunky way possible. The original is perfect in its simplicity so any attempts to augment it are doomed to failure but this seems like a particularly spectacularly big doom. It might be the kind of thing that is acceptable to a boozed-up, pilled-up festival crowd but for home listening, it is just not right. It makes me squirm every time I hear it.

'Incubus' starts off quite eerily and has some interesting snippets of dialogue in it but just as you start to warm to the music after the previous insult, it is suddenly drastically undermined by someone trying to impersonate late period Vangelis in a very bland manner and dominating the sound mix throughout.

'Aphorism' is an inoffensive short number with some chopped vocal samples about science and art accompanied by what does sound like a harpsichord but is no doubt some electronic trickery.

'Vortex' is another false start. Beginning with a fast pulse and some nice synth sounds, it feels like a fun, brisk number initially. After two minutes it appears to turn into a piano led ballad with humdrum drums and suddenly at around three minutes an awful bit of guitar and clumsy synths kick in. It sounds less cosmic and more like the rejected theme tune for an ignominiously failed TV pilot detective show from 1994. Everybody seems to be playing at once but not in synchronisation. It's a blessed relief when it ends.

'Regenerations' is a piece that segues together three different versions of the *Doctor Who* theme. It starts off with Delia Derbyshire's version and the Radiophonic Workshop gingerly added a few timid augmentations before it segues off into their own brand new arrangement of the theme. As someone who would love the TV show to have an all-electronic arrangement of the theme, I was really excited to find out what they could up with. The excitement turned to bitter disappointment. The keyboard sounds are bland, dreary and heavy handed. It fails to take off in any way and it is a merciful release when it segues into the Peter Howell arrangement of the theme.

It's not all misery, though, as it ends with the twenty minute 'ΔV' which goes through lots of changing phases of strange and enjoyable electronic sound. . It definitely feels less like everyone all joining it at once and more like everybody having some room to operate and contribute without getting messy. It builds in intensity until about half way through it becomes quite hard and intense (albeit beatless). This builds up to some scratchy guitar riffs and pounding drums and just as you're worried it's about to go off the boil, a hum of white noise comes in as the drums and guitars start backtracking. Suddenly it's pounding drums and an electronic breakbeat with lots of lovely abstract electronics.

So, not a complete turd of album by any means, it's at its best when creating experimental music and at its worst as it goes towards the mainstream. Unfortunately, at its very worst it is actually unbearable. Given the circumstances of its release, I think it best to give them the benefit of the doubt as their live shows do feature some interesting new material. Hopefully the album that hits the shops will be much, much better – in fact, it almost certainly will as it most likely won't have their version of 'Ziwzih Ziwzih OO-OO-OO' on it.

2015

DAPHNE ORAM – POP TRYOUTS
Label: Mondo Hebden
IS: MH1

This release was actually borne out of a book – this one, in fact.
    While going through Daphne Oram's papers at Goldsmiths at the University of London, as part of my research, I was offered the chance to listen to her archive which they had handily stored on an mp3 player. So, popping on my headphones and listening while I worked, one particular piece leapt out at me. Apparently the original tape was labelled 'Pop Tryouts' and it contained multiple takes on a particular piece of the 'Birds of Parralax' suite that appears on the *Oramics* compilation. As I'd just started doing a tape label, I couldn't help but

think this was the sort of thing that would never appear on any sort of compilation CD as it was too long and that the only way it could see the light of day would be if someone like me put it out on a cheap, simple format like tape...

I think when it got to the part where Daphne starts performing an acapella version of the track that I knew I had to do this. It's fascinating to hear all her different takes and approaches to the track, both as a genuine insight into her work but also because it's one of my favourite tracks by her.

It's on side two of the tape, however, that things begin to get very strange with one very minimalist take, one that sounds like Oram playing the melody on hooting owl toy with a melancholy shuffling slowed-down percussion beat and the aforementioned acapella version with whistles and taps. It would be unfair of me to endorse something I released myself too strongly but I had some wonderful feedback from people who bought the tape. Intriguingly, the original tape from Daphne's archive ended with a recording of the initial BBC version of 'Time Beat' which makes you wonder if the piece takes inspiration from 'Time Beat'?

JOHN BAKER – THE VENDETTA TAPES
Label: Buried Treasure
ID: BUTR8

Following Trunk Record's two CD career spanning overview, we now have this more in depth release focused almost entirely on John's soundtrack work for tough guy thriller *Vendetta*. Like *The Baker Tapes* it has been compiled by Alan Gubby but this time coming out on Alan's own label, the recently started Buried Treasure.

It's important to bear in mind that John Baker was not just a Radiophonic Workshop composer but was also a classically trained pianist and a jazz musician. What is so wonderful about his *Vendetta* soundtrack (which was featured twice on Volume 1 of *The Baker Tapes*) is how it brought together these three strands. Sometimes the electronics are accompanied by flute, trumpet, double bass and a very nimble jazz drummer and sometimes we can hear Mr. Baker at the piano. The soundtrack provides all the moods you would expect for that kind of show; dark menace, moody stillness, iconic streetwalking music and fighting jazz. It's just that Baker's arrangements are light years ahead. Plenty of composers these days do try to blend jazz, classical and electronics but they never come close because Baker was a towering genius of all three, they were his lifeblood and he nails it here in a way nobody else ever has. It's almost ruthlessly inventive, flipping the clichés of 1960s action soundtrack and deserves to hold its head up high alongside peers like *Get Carter*.

Yet, Gubby is not content just to give us a lost classic of 60s soundtracks. He then goes and adds a load of bonus tracks from the John Baker Radiophonic archive, providing a nice contrast to the tough sound of *Vendetta* with far more electronic work ranging from Baker's trademark bright and breezy melodies to staggering alienated minimalism. It's the sort of stuff a more ruthless label could have gotten away with holding back for a separate release and charging us double but Gubby's unmistakable passion for the material forces him to make this the best package possible. I have only heard the digital version to date so I can only comment on the remastering for that but it is perfect.

The only downside of this album is it leaves the listener hungry for more and the fact that someone can put such a focused but brilliant album in 2015 makes you wonder what else is out there. By my fifth listen I was left desperately craving a massive box set. You owe it to yourself to buy this both to treat yourself and to support the work of those who continue to dig up gold like this for us.

BRIAN GASCOIGNE, DESMOND BRISCOE, DAVID VORHAUS & STOMU YAMASHTA – PHASE IV
Label: Waxworks
ID: WW008

Tracklist
1 – Phase I
2 – Phase II
3 – Phase III
4 – Phase IV

Thanks to the current boom in demand for horror, sci-fi and cult movie soundtracks, all sorts of unusual oddities are coming out on deluxe heavyweight vinyl with stunning new artwork. From this wave of releases comes the soundtrack for semi-obscure 1974 giant ant movie *Phase IV*. While not well known by any means, it is notable as being the only full length film made by Saul Bass, the visual artist behind many classic logos and film posters.

There are a few names credited on here. It says that Gascoigne did the main score, Yamashta did the 'montages' and Briscoe/Vorhaus are credited with the electronic sounds. However, for this release, everything has been segued together into four pieces (simply called Phases I-IV) which makes distinguishing individual contributions a little tricky. This method of track-listing works wonderfully from a listener's perspective, creating a real album feel rather than just an endless collection of cues. It also evokes the film and its many different (and strange) moods far more clearly. It's just a big nuisance if you want to know who you are listening to. There was a good quality CD bootleg of the soundtrack a few years ago that separated the tracks but it didn't provide any clear track-listing.

There is a main theme with a mix of dramatic strings and fuzzy Morricone-esque guitar. Then there are some parts that definitely have a very Vorhaus feel with their dark, moody analogue synths and thudding rhythms but how do we know who it is? Maybe Gascoigne had some synths? He was in a band with Yamashta, after all, so maybe they did some parts together? Is it Briscoe and Vorhaus working together in tandem? Is it library music recorded by Vorhaus being used? What did Desmond do?

With both Briscoe and the film maker no longer around to tell us, we can only guess. One particularly interesting part is a piece of electronic sound that sounds exactly like a piece created at the Workshop. Perhaps it is Desmond Briscoe providing a very accurate 'cover version' for the film?

It is an album that raises many, many questions about what we are actually enjoying but the important part is we ARE enjoying it. At the time of writing it was still on sale from the label and several stockists but like all modern vinyl runs it will be quite limited.

NOTES

1 "BBC's Radiophonic Workshop", *The Times*, 24 May 1958
2 Schaeffer, Pierre, Journal entry for 15 May 1948, quoted in Kane, Brian, *Sound Unseen: Acousmatic Sound in Theory and Practice*, p16
3 ibid
4 http://www.stockhausen.org/tape_loops.html
5 ibid
6 ibid
7 Letter to Henri Posseur, quoted in Toop, Richard, "Stockhausen's Konkrete Etüde", *The Music Review* 37, no. 4 (November 1976), p.297
8 Maconie, Robin, *Other Planets: The Music of Karlheinz Stockhausen*, Scarecrow Press (2005), p.106
9 Hiller, Lejaren, *Report on Contemporary Music 1961, Experimental Music Studio* (1962), p.59
10 "Poeme Electronique by Edgard Varese comes as close as any work to being a masterpiece of this type of music" - Hoffer, Charles, *Western Music Listening Today*, Cengage Learning Inc. (2009), p.304
11 http://news.bbc.co.uk/1/hi/uk/2669735.stm
12 http://daphneoram.org/bbc-click-feature-the-beginnings-of-electronic-music/
13 *Wee Have Also Sound-Houses*, radio documentary, 3 August 2008
14 Meetings held on 14th December 1956, 6th March 1956 and 10th December 1957, minutes held in BBC Written Archives, Caversham
15 Letter from Samuel Beckett to Donald McWhinnie, BBC Written Archive
16 Kevin Branigan, *Radio Beckett: Musicality in the Radio Plays of Samuel Beckett*, p. 90
17 Oram collection, Goldsmiths, University of London
18 MRG Garrard, 1957 report to the BBC, cited in Richard Holligum, *Between Two Worlds - The Pre-History and Formation*

of the BBC Radiophonic Workshop (Doctoral thesis, University of Northampton, 2013)
19 Internal memos, BBC Written Archives, Caversham
20 Undated memo from Daphne Oram, held in BBC Written Archives, Caversham
21 Roy Curtis-Bramwell, *The BBC Radiophonic Workshop: the first 25 years : the inside story of providing sound and music for television and radio, 1958-1983*, p.19
22 Undated note from Daphne Oram, held in the Oram Collection, Goldsmiths, University of London
23 Quoted in Louis Niebur, *Special Sound*, p.29
24 Quoted in Curtis-Bramwell, op cit, p.22
25 Daphne Oram, letter held in the Oram Collection, Goldsmiths, University of London
26 Sean Street, *The Poetry of Radio, the Colour of Sound*
27 Memo to Robin Midgley, BBC Written Archive, Caversham
28 http://genome.ch.bbc.co.uk/d774deab7ae344e6850212469799 c327
29 Letter from Daphne Oram to the BBC, held in the Oram Collection, Goldsmiths, University of London
30 The widely reported figure of three months has never been definitely traced to a specific source. Brian Hodgson commented that it originated with a brain surgeon friend of one of the Committee who oversaw the setting up of the workshop, but which brain surgeon and which committee member remains unknown. Dick Mills claims six months in the Wee Also Have Sound Houses documentary but attributes it to "the BBC in their infinite wisdom" and "health & safety". Mill's six months figure seems much more likely with the Workshop opening in May and Daphne quitting in November and I have consequently gone with that.
31 Copy held in the Oram Collection, Goldsmiths, University of London
32 Quoted in Curtis-Bramwell, op cit, p137
33 ibid

34 Letter from Spike Milligan to The Listener, April 1970, and reply from Desmond Briscoe, May 1970
35 Roy Curtis-Bramwell, *The first 25 years*, p.21
36 Colm McAuliffe, Interview with Dick Mills, 19th September 2014, http://thequietus.com/articles/16273-radiophonic-workshop-interview
37 Giles Oakley, oration at Maddalena Fagandini's funeral, reported at http://ex-bbc.net/cgi-bin/yabb/YaBB.pl?num=1354625297
38 Oakley, ibid
39 Interview with weheelmeout.com, June 2014
40 Sonic Boom, Interview with Delia Derbyshire, *Surface* magazine, May 2000
41 ibid
42 Delia Derbyshire, interviewed by John Cavanagh, "Delia Derbyshire: On Our Wavelength", in *Boazine* 7, reprinted on delia-derbyshire.net
43 Author telephone interview with Brian Hodgson, August 2015
44 Cavanagh interview, ibid
45 Author telephone interview with Sonic Boom, 2014
46 Jo Hutton, "Radiophonic Ladies", Sonic Arts Network, February 2000
47 Author telephone interview with Sonic Boom, 2014
48 Author telephone interview with Brian Hodgson, August 2015
49 For example, https://archive.org/details/IsaacAsimov-TheFoundationTrilogy
50 Franklin Crawford, "Robert Moog, Ph.D. '64, inventor of the music synthesizer, dies of brain cancer", Cornell University News Service, August 23, 2005 (http://www.news.cornell.edu/stories/2005/08/robert-moog-dies-71)
51 http://www.vintagesynth.com/misc/vcs3.php
52 Hayward, Philip and Fitzgerald, Jon, 'Musical Engagements with the British TV Series *Doctor Who*, in *Music in Science Fiction Television*, p.136

53 He later regretted the decision, and admitted he was wrong to do so in his biography, *Who and Me*
54 Author interview with Ray White, June 2015
55 This description on the original flyer contained an asterisk at the end, which directed the reader to this definition of the word ENTERTAINMENT – 'a performance which delights'. The flyer itself can be viewed online at http://whitefiles.org/rwg/index6.html
56 Flyer, ibid
57 Desmond Briscoe, cited in Roy Curtis-Bramwell, *The first 25 years*, quoted at http://wikidelia.net/wiki/I.E.E.100
58 According to Hodgson 'I don't think she ever forgave me for that.' (Louis Neibur interview with Hodgson, quoted at http://wikidelia.net/wiki/I.E.E.100
59 'Radiophonic Ladies' by Jo Hutton, archived at http://delia-derbyshire.net/sites/ARTICLE2000JoHutton.html
60 The Gulbenkian Foundation is an international institution based in Portugal who fund developments in cultural, educational, social and scientific interests.
61 Author interview with Elizabeth Parker, May 2014
62 Author interview with Brian Hodgson, August 2014
63 ibid
64 Author interview with Brian Hodgson, August 2014
65 Footnotes to Fit the Seventh, in Douglas Adams, *The Hitchhiker's Guide to the Galaxy: The Original Radio Scripts* (second edition), Pan Books, 2003
66 http://whitefiles.org/rws/r04.htm
67 Author interview with Brian Hodgson, August 2014
68 http://whitefiles.org/rws/r03.htm
69 Cited in Ray White, *BBC Radiophonic Workshop*, p.31
70 Author interview with Elizabeth Parker, May 2014
71 Letter from Daphne Oram to Roy Curtis-Bramwell, 3rd December 1983, Oram Archives, Goldsmiths, University of London
72 Letter from Francis to Oram, held in the Oram Collection, Goldsmiths, University of London
73 Jean Seaton, *Pinkoes and Traitors*

74 Dr Andrius Bielskis and Dr Kelvin Knight, *Virtue and Economy: Essays on Morality and Markets*
75 Author interview with Elizabeth Parker, May 2014
76 Author interview with Ray White, 2015
77 Author interview with Elizabeth Parker, May 2014
78 Dick Mills, in *Wee Have Also Sound-Houses*, BBC Radio, 2008
79 Author interview with Sonic Boom, 2015
80 Author interview with Brian Hodgson, August 2014
81 ibid
82 Brian Hodgson, 'Musique Concrete for the Masses! Reflections of a sound pioneer', in *Wheel Me Out: The Anthology*
83 Author interview with Sonic Boom, 2015
84 ibid
85 Author interview with Brian Hodgson, August 2014
86 Quoted in Mark Brend, *Strange Sounds*, p.70
87 Author interview with Elizabeth Parker, May 2014
88 Author interview with Brian Hodgson, August 2014
89 *Giants of Steam*, BBC One, 21 May 1963. Narrated by John Slater and directed by John Read.
90 No less a composer than Steve Reich worked to similar effect on *Different Trains* in 1990
91 Duncan's other work includes collaborations with Benjamin Britten, the English Stage Company and the script for cult movie *Girl On A Motorcycle*
92 Rising Storm website, review of ITHICA, 'A Game for all who Know'
93 Author interview with Brian Hodgson, August 2014
94 Between 2006 and 2008, the album was reissued with new cover artwork depicting Delia Derbyshire, leading many to wrongly attribute it solely to Delia.
95 *A Movie For Daddy* (Scores To Groove The Screens By Blue Note)
96 Author of *Chariot of the Gods* and others, positing an extraterrestrial origin for Mankind.
97 *I Am The Center: Private Issue New Age Music In America 1950-1990* (Light In The Attic, 2013)

SELECT BIBLIOGRAPHY

- Bielskis, Andrius and Knight, Kelvin, *Virtue and Economy: Essays on Morality and Markets* (Ashgate, 2015)
- Born, Georgina, *Uncertain Vision: Birt, Dyke and the Reinvention of the BBC* (Martin, Secker & Warberg, 2004)
- Branigan, Kevin, *Radio Beckett: Musicality in the Radio Plays of Samuel Beckett*, (Peter Lang AG, 2008)
- Brend, Mark, *Strange Sounds: Offbeat Instruments and Sonic Experiments in Pop* (Backbeat Books, 2005)
- Curtis-Bramwell, Roy and Briscoe, Desmond, *The BBC Radiophonic Workshop: the first 25 years : the inside story of providing sound and music for television and radio, 1958-1983*, (BBC, 1983)
- Donnelly, K.J (ed). *Music in Science Fiction Television* (Routledge, 2013)
- Hiller, Lejaren, *Report on Contemporary Music 1961*, (Experimental Music Studio, 1962)
- Hoffer, Charles, *Western Music Listening Today*, (Wadsworth Publishing Co Inc, 4th ed, 2009)

- Holligum, Richard, *Between Two Worlds - The Pre-History and Formation of the BBC Radiophonic Workshop* (Doctoral thesis, University of Northampton, 2013)
- Kane, Brian, *Sound Unseen: Acousmatic Sound in Theory and Practice*, (OUP USA, 2014)
- Letts, Barry, *Who and Me* (BBC Audiobooks, 2008)
- Maconie, Robin, *Other Planets: The Music of Karlheinz Stockhausen* (Scarecrow Press, 2005)
- Milligan Spike, *Man of Letters* (Penguin, 2014)
- Niebur, Louis, *Special Sound, The Creation and Legacy of the BBC Radiophonic Workshop*, (OUP, 2010)
- Oram, Daphne, *Individual Note of Music, Sound and Electronics* (Galliard, 1972)
- Powell, Mike, *I Am The Center: Private Issue New Age Music In America 1950-1990* (Light In The Attic, 2013)
- Schaeffer, Pierre, *In Search of a Concrete Music* (University of California Press, 2013)
- Seaton, Jean, *Pinkoes and Traitors* (Profile Books, 2015)
- Street, Sean, *The Poetry of Radio, the Colour of Sound*, (Routledge, 2013)
- *Wheel Me Out: The Anthology* (iTunes)
- White, Ray, *BBC Radiophonic Workshop: An Engineer's Perspective* (http://whitefiles.org/rwx/rws2.pdf)